# A SUNNY
# PLACE
# FOR
# SHADY
# PEOPLE

Sardinia
(ITALY)

I T A L Y

Italia
Penins

Aeolian Islands

Aegadian
Islands

Strait of Sicily

Sicily
(ITALY)

TUNIS

Pantelleria
(ITALY)

Malta Channel

VALLETTA

Pelagie Islands
(ITALY)

MALTA

TUNISIA

Kerkennah
Islands

M E D I T E R R A N E A N
S E A

Djerba

0        100 km
0           100 mi

TRIPOLI

L I B Y A

# A SUNNY PLACE FOR SHADY PEOPLE

*How Malta Became One of the Most*
*Curious and Corrupt Places in the World*

## Ryan Murdock

TRINITY UNIVERSITY PRESS
San Antonio, Texas

Trinity University Press
San Antonio, Texas 78212

Copyright © 2024 by Ryan Murdock

Book design by BookMatters
Jacket design by Derek Thornton / Notch Design
Cover art: Stocksy images 1069210, 1237861, 5048448
Images: iStock/Peter Hermes Furian (frontis); Tomoko Goto (author photo and
part pages)

Image captions: Part 1, Valletta, Malta; part 2, Zejtun shop window; part 3, Zejtun
village streets; part 4, Saint Ursula Street, Valletta; part 5, detail of carnival float
mocking Malta's passport program

ISBN 978-1-59534-294-2 hardcover
ISBN 978-1-59534-295-9 ebook

Printed in Canada

Trinity University Press strives to produce its books using methods and materials
in an environmentally sensitive manner. We favor working with manufacturers
that practice sustainable management of all-natural resources, produce paper
using recycled stock, and manage forests with the best possible practices for
people, biodiversity, and sustainability. The press is a member of the Green Press
Initiative, a nonprofit program dedicated to supporting publishers in their efforts
to reduce their impacts on endangered forests, climate change, and forest-
dependent communities.

The paper used in this publication meets the minimum requirements of the
American National Standard for Information Sciences—Permanence of Paper
for Printed Library Materials, ANSI 39.48–1992.

CIP data on file at the Library of Congress

28    27    26    25    24    ◉    5    4    3    2    1

*For T.G. & D.*

# CONTENTS

# PROLOGUE

I was visiting family in Canada when I got a late-evening text from my wife on October 16, 2017: "They killed Daphne with bomb."

"Daphne" was Daphne Caruana Galizia, an independent Maltese journalist whose investigations into government corruption had made her a target of the country's rich and powerful—especially the ruling Labour Party, which saw her as its only real opposition. The last story she had written was about a court appearance by the prime minister's chief of staff, Keith Schembri, earlier that day. It ended with the words: "There are crooks everywhere you look now. The situation is desperate." She published her article, closed her laptop, and stood up to go to the bank, where she'd been cashing checks on her husband's account because hers was still frozen by the economy minister.

Before leaving her peaceful hilltop home surrounded by gardens in rural Bidnija, she set a plate of tomatoes and mozzarella in front of her oldest son, Matthew, a data journalist who had shared a Pulitzer Prize as part of the International Consortium of Investigative Journalists that broke the Panama Papers, an exposé of the secret world of offshore tax havens. The two were sifting through a database of 11.5 million leaked financial and legal records to figure out why two top government officials opened companies in Panama within days of the Labour Party's election to power.

She ran out the door, then rushed back in to grab her checkbook. "Okay, I'm really going this time," she said, smiling at Matthew. The explosion happened minutes after she drove away. She was fifty-three years old.

A neighbor who saw Daphne driving down the hill toward him told police he immediately sensed that something was wrong. "She appeared to be panicking," he said. "I heard a small bang, like fireworks. Then I heard a piercing scream."

The first explosion tore off her leg and scattered debris nearby, but she'd only just begun to scream when, seconds later, a larger explosion engulfed her car in a ball of fire.

"I saw parts of her ripped off," the neighbor said. "Her hand flew off. It was terrible. Then I saw blood…I realized they were human parts. I could do nothing. It was so cruel."

The blast shook the house where Matthew was hunched over his laptop. He ran out the door in a panic and saw a column of black smoke boiling into the sky from somewhere down the hill. His legs were shaking so badly he could barely run. The road was on fire when he reached the scene, where bloody pieces of his mother were scattered across a field.

The car's horn continued to blare as he ran back and forth, frantic but unable to approach the inferno. He was looking for something to pry open the door when he saw a severed leg on the ground. Two young police officers arrived minutes later. One grabbed a fire extinguisher and ran toward the smoke but then stopped and dropped it on the ground. Matthew tried to take it from him, screaming, "What are you doing? What are you doing?" The officer placed a hand on his shoulder and said, "There's nothing we can do." As they stood there watching the car go up in flames, the other policeman began to cry.

Firefighters and Civil Protection Department officials described finding a person inside the burning car and pieces of flesh scattered around the bomb site, including "a leg ripped apart from the thigh." Civil protection officer Frank Sammut said, "I saw a human hand on the passenger side and a burning figure inside. Nothing could be done." Firefighters would return two days later to chop down a tree so investigators could search its branches for human remains.

Photos of Daphne's burned body parts were circulated on WhatsApp and other digital messaging services within hours of her death. They were taken at the crime scene, evidently by police. At around the same time, Police sergeant Raymond Mifsud posted a message to his Facebook page that read, "Everyone gets what they deserve, cow dung! Feeling happy :)"

He would eventually be suspended with pay but never dismissed. Loyalists in closed Labour Party Facebook groups, whose membership included senior government officials, celebrated her death with statements like "*ma tistax rip ghax saret bicciet lanqas tista titqaleb ahseb u ara carma is a bich* [sic]" (She can't rest in peace because she's in pieces, she can't even be buried, karma is a bitch).

The killing made headlines around the world as readers with no understanding of Malta tried to make sense of the targeted murder of a journalist in a European Union member state. Prime Minister Joseph Muscat appeared on CNN, where he told Christiane Amanpour he would "leave no stone unturned" in finding out who killed the woman he described as his "harshest critic." He seemed to have difficulty suppressing a smirk as he spoke. His wife was more direct in an exclusive media interview nine months later. "If there is someone who wants Daphne Caruana Galizia to be alive today, that is me,"

Michelle Muscat said. "When I heard the news about what happened to her, I think I was more sorry than her own family. Her family could go on to make her a saint; but at the time I said to myself, 'Now I will have to live with her lies.' I want her alive."

The prime minister issued his official statement as the shell of Daphne's car lay smoldering in a field. "Everyone is aware that Ms. Caruana Galizia was one of my harshest critics, politically and personally, as she was for others, too," he wrote. "However, I can never use, in any way, this fact to justify, in any possible way, this barbaric act that goes against civilization and all dignity."

Within days protesters besieged his office at the Auberge de Castille, demanding justice for Daphne and an end to the impunity at the heart of his corruption-plagued administration. His response was to fly to Dubai to promote Malta's controversial citizenship-by-investment program, known on the island as cash-for-passports.

From 2011 to 2017 I led a secluded life in small villages on the island of Malta. To the casual visitor, Malta is a sleepy place of sun-soaked shorelines and fortified harbors, an island of busy cafés and grilled fish dinners with chilled white wine. And it was—on the surface.

In the beginning I found the cultural clashes of island life comical, as the small hidden assumptions both Maltese and foreigner made about one another revealed misunderstandings that verged on the surreal. Heated emotions gave way to shrugs and laughter as the best-laid plans always seemed to go wrong. There was something endearing about the way cobbled-together solutions eventually worked out. We lived surrounded by every era of European history in an easygoing place where bureaucratic rules and minor traffic laws could be safely ignored. The kindness of friends outweighed the frustrations of trying to get things done in a society where reliability depended on someone else's whims.

But this sunny surface concealed dark undercurrents that expressed themselves through car bombs and systemic corruption. I watched as an organized criminal network took over the government of a European Union member state with the widespread support of its citizens. The seeds of this takeover were deeply embedded in the culture, ingrained in a worldview called amoral familism, and stirred to festering malignancy under the leadership of Prime Minister Dom Mintoff. But it was Joseph Muscat who transformed the tiny island nation into a kleptocracy.

On that timeless, sun-struck rock in the middle of the Sicily Channel, things go on changing, but they mostly stay the same. The clues to what came later were there in every village interaction. All it took was someone rash enough to rip out the brakes. This is the story of what I saw.

*Note:* The names and identifying details of my friends have been changed to protect their privacy. Our conversations, and the insights they shared with me, are reproduced from memory and notes made after the fact. The details of corruption recounted here have been widely reported on the island. The names of historical figures, politicians, criminals, and alleged criminals remain the same.

# ONE

# ISLAND

# LIFE

# FIRST PROMISE
# OF THE SOUTH

The descent began around the middle of Sicily, with the lights of Palermo off to the right and hills all April green below. And then the turquoise waters of the coast abruptly gave way to deep blue broken by the white froth of wave tops. The plane continued to descend—I felt it in my ears and saw it in the spinning altitude numbers on the monitor—but still the blue went on. It continued deep blue for another twenty minutes, away from Europe, toward North Africa, long after I'd begun to wonder if we overshot our mark and should prepare for a water landing. But then the island of Gozo appeared: green in winter, with geological bones poking through; barren in summer, burned brown and so bleak you could be forgiven for believing that the pilot struck land near Tripoli.

That first glimpse was one of shock. Beyond brief Gozo with its scattered towns, and uninhabited Comino with its bathers and picture-postcard turquoise pools, Malta rose up like a Moroccan hill town or a Brazilian favela. I could almost see the entire island at once, and even from several thousand feet I could see how badly overbuilt it was. Somewhere deep in my gut I had a nagging feeling that moving there had been a mistake. But my wife and I had already given up our rental house in Canada, sold the furniture, and quit stable jobs. We'd simply have to see it through. We got off the plane at the country's sole airport, whose runway cut across an eighth of the island.

Cars rushed past in both directions, seemingly without end. We hurtled through dusty villages of a numbing sameness, their outskirts blending into those of the next town in this continuous urban sprawl of half-finished concrete shells seen through a haze of diesel fumes. Streets gaped as though they'd been bombed. Masonry crashed, concrete dust floated in the air, and the clatter of pneumatic drills competed with car horns and shouting to create a staggering wall of sound. Large billboards dominated the roadsides and obscured what little there was to see beyond the monotonous identical buildings. The roads were a maze of potholes and bad patch jobs, terribly congested, with a heavy stink of exhaust. There was litter everywhere.

The architecture of Malta was a uniform yellowish tan, like ancient sand or aging Limburger cheese. This is because both the buildings and the hills were carved from stone. The broad streets of Valletta were embellished, Baroque, but the typical town was a monotony of identical stone cubes, identical carved balustrades, identical winding alleys, and identical blocks of modern flats thrown up on the outskirts like chicken coops, many of which were abandoned half-built. Only the churches differed, but chiefly in terms of scale. They were all built according to the same Baroque style, similar to churches in neighboring Sicily, with large domes and belfries that dominated every village skyline. Each contained the carved wooden effigy of a saint, and in each church the same old ladies sat through the same rituals in the same black shawls. The outsider could be forgiven if they lost track of which inland village they'd stumbled upon.

Where were the magnificent views of limestone cliffs and azure seas that completely dominated any online image search? Most of the accessible shoreline was heavily urbanized, taken over by hotels, ramshackle apartment blocks, and squatters' shacks.

Malta itself is roughly 20 miles long and 12 miles wide. At 122 square miles (316 square km), it is smaller than the Isle of Wight in the United Kingdom or Martha's Vineyard in the United States. Some 545,000 people call this tiny rock home, making it the European Union's most densely populated country and, at 1,672 people per square kilometer, one of the most densely populated countries in the world.

Climb above the island in a small plane and you would see an oblong rock, capped by the anvil of Mellieħa and the Marfa Ridge at the Gozo end, with the deep fingers of the Grand Harbour and Marsamxett gouged out, and the bite of Marsaxlokk Bay in the south. The land on the eastern side leans toward the sea, as though all those towns and villages were weighing it down. The sparsely populated African-facing coast rises higher, to the sheer cliffs of Dingli and the Ħal Far heights of Ħasan's Cave. The north is completely bisected by the Great Fault, a steep upthrust ridge where the British built their long defensive wall, the Victoria Lines, manned for a while but never assailed. The island's only peak is Mount Magħtab, a smoldering landfill, already overfull.

Most of Malta is composed of sedimentary limestone that formed underwater some 200 million years ago as shells, coral, and sediment were compacted beneath the weight of the sea. The islands that we see today are the barren remnants of eroded mountaintops, separated from Sicily at the end of the Ice Age by cataclysmic floods. Five different layers can be distinguished, and they show different phases in the development of the Mediterranean: Upper Coraline Limestone, Greensand, Blue Clay, Globigerina Limestone, and Lower Coraline Limestone. After emerging from the waves like foam-born Aphrodite, the island was shaped by tectonic activity, sea, wind, rain, and now people—far too many people.

The landscape presents a bleak face to a cruel, desiccating sun.

Stony, steep, and poorly watered, this is a country of garigue patched by pockets of agricultural land. At first glance the rock overshadowed any remaining trees—stunted olive, tamarisk, and carob trees and the ever-present prickly pear. You had to look closely to see the rock thistle, rosemary, brambles, and thyme.

Malta has no permanent creeks or rivers. Natural water is scarce and heavily used, and so the islanders have always relied on the winter rains to fill their rock-cut cisterns. But even this was no longer enough, and reverse-osmosis facilities squeeze desalinated life from the sea. In the hot, dry summer, which lasts from May to September, those seas were calm and inviting, and later bathtub warm. But in winter storms lashed the coasts, bringing fierce winds that tore at the houses and ferocious green waves that ripped chunks of stone from the cliffs and hurled them into the sea.

Throughout most of its history, the Maltese people were poor and nature was stingy. There are no natural resources to sell or exploit, and no manufacturing of any importance or scale. Life had always been a struggle, and the island had never been able to sustain itself without help. Its parched limestone formed a barren, porous landscape that soaked up blood and conquerors; that took and took until there was nothing left; that gave little, and grudgingly.

An island like that is a self-contained world, a place you can map and know in its entirety, but it is also a place defined by boundaries, a nested landscape—both literal and metaphorical—of small orderly worlds. Because they are small, islands are also infinitely divisible; small boundaries and small differences matter more.

I knew nothing about Malta when we decided to move there, just its location and a vague impression that it had something to do with knights. It was two hundred miles from Tunis, practically in the Gulf of Tripoli, and farther south than the northernmost point of Tunisia.

A place so remote that few could identify it as a country, even fewer locate it on a map.

I first touched the Mediterranean through the writings of Lawrence Durrell. I was living in Tokyo in my late twenties teaching English—the farthest place you could imagine from what he was describing. In a tiny apartment where I could reach out and touch both walls, shaken by passing trucks, I read about the spirit of place and how everyone has a personal landscape, a landscape that resonates with them on some deep tuning-fork level. That's where your thoughts are most lucid, and, for a writer, it's where you do your best work.

Born in colonial India in the foothills of the Himalayas but sent to boarding school in England, Durrell hated the buttoned-up lifestyle of the North. When his father died, he saw an opportunity to escape. Somehow, by some incredible art of persuasion, he convinced his mother to pack up their entire family—four children, of which he was the eldest—and move them to the Greek island of Corfu. They lived a crazy island life with eccentric locals and writers dropping by—people like Freya Stark and Patrick Leigh Fermor—and during all those years Durrell plugged away in a little stone house on the side of a mountain and taught himself to write.

I fell in love with that rugged, stony Mediterranean landscape on trips to Croatia and the south of France, with the garigue and the olive tree, and that strange translucent light. I was drawn to the café culture and wine-soaked intellectual stimulation, with its hint of past empires and layers of civilization ghosted over everything. I imagined myself living in a quiet old house among olive trees and vineyards, eating heavy bread and drinking coarse local wines. Swimming naked in the velvet sea. Talking to old men in shabby coats and berets over early-morning coffee and anisette. But it had to be a place that hadn't been written about so I could contribute something new. I'd written a book about a long overland journey through Central America, and I'd been writing feature articles for a Canadian travel magazine for more than six years, but those stories involved constant motion. It was time to cultivate deeper roots.

That Durrellian image of island life never left me when we went back to Ontario to be closer to my ailing father in 2002. I ground out a living working for temp agencies by day and writing at night, and when my small online publishing business began earning enough money for us to live on after ten years of bare subsistence, I decided it was time to experience this spirit of place for myself. I mentioned the idea to my wife, Tomoko, who had shared my journey since we were university students.

"It would mean giving notice on the house and relocating the cat," she said. "And I would have to quit my job. Should I really give up translation? For what?"

I looked out the window at the dull gray, southern Ontario winter. "It isn't like we'd be leaving much behind." The monotonous low-level rage of Toronto traffic. The cultural death of blandly identical suburban commuter towns.

So we contacted a moving company, which came to collect our belongings. "I'll send you an address in a couple of weeks," I told them. And we were off to find a house in a country we'd never visited. I thought I'd spend four or five years there writing an upbeat island book inspired by Durrell. I never imagined we would leave under such a black cloud.

We rented a sprawling old house—a small palazzo in island parlance—in the village of Zejtun, deep in the island's south. Zejtun took its name from the Sicilian Arabic word for olive. There weren't many olive trees in Malta anymore, but the production of oil was once an important industry. Zejtun's recorded history went back eight hundred years. It played a pivotal role in the Great Siege of 1565, when

Ottoman forces landed nearby in the area of Marsaxlokk and were quickly engaged by the local militia, and it continued to be attacked by Turkish pirates until 1614. It was raised to the status of town by the island's last grand master of the Knights of Malta, Ferdinand von Hompesch, in 1797.

The town's geography was elevated as well, situated as it was on a hill that rose sixty meters above sea level, with the village of Tarxien to the north and, beyond a few cultivated fields bordered by dry stone walls and wild growths of prickly pear, the industrial zone of Bulebel, where De La Rue printed money for various nations and other companies made cables and packaging materials. But the area's ties to industry went back much further. At the southern edge of Zejtun, the grounds of Saint Thomas More Secondary School had been turned into an archaeological excavation. The remains of a Roman villa were found there in 1961, with traces of original tile and colored stucco, and carved stone channels that bore silent testament to a sizable olive oil industry in the vicinity. Another Roman villa had been uncovered in nearby Wied Żembaq, on the outskirts of Birżebbuġa, and the area around our town was riddled with Punic tombs.

We were living in the oldest part of the village, the "upper town" zones called Ħal Bisbut and Ħal Ġwann, where the streets were built in the medieval style with narrow, winding alleys and arched arcades leading to hidden houses and quiet gardens. It was only by exploring them on foot that I noticed the Arab influence hiding behind the more obvious curves of Baroque balconies.

Malta lacked timber for housing, but the island was blessed with an abundance of good building stone that is soft enough to be easily worked. Traditional methods of architecture—corbel and stone slab roofs, external cantilevered stairways, and the waterproofing of roofs using a mixture of lime-based mortar with *pozzolana*, or crushed pottery—appear to have been transplanted to the islands directly from North Africa or the Levant. Such corbel roofs are not seen on the nearby islands of Sicily, Lampedusa, or Pantelleria, and the use of archaic Arabic terms, such as *kileb* for corbel, seem to have links from as far off as Jordan. Arabic-derived terms are still in use to describe the components of traditional dwellings: house (*dar*), courtyard (*bitha*), well (*bir*), alley (*sqaq*), and market (*suq*).

The distinctive wooden balconies projecting from the upper story of older homes—*il-Gallarija*, with their windows and brightly painted wood—have become a tourist symbol of Malta, but few realize they predate the Knights and the Italian Baroque. Their ancestor is the North African *muxrabija*, the latticed peephole window that gave views of the street and cooling breezes to cloistered women across the Maghreb. Lattice had simply morphed into glass as the Arab centuries receded, and as women were no longer locked away from the prying eyes of the outside world.

The early village houses echoed the squat stone farmhouses (*razzett*) of the countryside: flat-roofed, thick-walled dwellings without windows on the lower story, and with a single entrance behind a strong door that was braced at night with heavy cast-iron rod latches (*staneg*). The entrance hall always led to a courtyard (*il-bitha*), the home's central feature, with a stone wellhead and reservoir beneath.

As parish churches went up in the village core, such houses clustered around them to form crooked lanes, radiating outward like cracks in a pane of glass, to the fields on the village periphery. Today those village fringes contain modern houses and shining white blocks of flats.

In the older parts of town, Christianity overwrote earlier Muslim North African roots like a palimpsest, creating a hybrid architecture of subtle contradiction. Our neighborhood was rich in corner shrines, statues of Christian saints in niches on the façades of houses. Each statue told a tale of struggle, or hope, or of powerful conviction, even unto death. These corner niches recalled the narrative of a collective mythology each time residents looked up while walking past. Perhaps they might remember to be a little kinder to their neighbor, or a little more patient in rush-hour traffic. Their great proliferation also reminded me of just what a hold the Catholic Church had over these islands, how much it controlled people's lives and daily routine and even their thoughts.

There were three different churches within earshot of my study, each competing like the voices in the street to drown each other out. The thrice-daily Angelus sounded like a fistful of coins falling on pavement. Other bells were sober and sonorous, while some sounded their praise in a frenzy of clanging. The worst were the practice sessions, when bell-ringing novices tried to learn a song. Predictably, none of the churches were in sync. Their bells chimed all the right hours at the wrong intervals.

They told me the worst was the *ċuqlajta*, a monotonous wooden clapper that replaced the bells on Good Friday and thundered from dawn to dark with the penitential insistence of a jackhammer at treble the volume. Only a few very traditional villages still tormented believers, nonbelievers, and small animals with this device, and ours happened to be one of them.

The writer Norman Douglas had spent time in Malta. In *Looking Back*, he wrote: "The bell-ringing of the Maltese bigots drove me nearly crazy; I cursed the British Government for allowing it to go on. I disliked the people, and thanked God I had not to live on their island for long." He must have been there for Easter.

# CAT LADIES AND SHRUGGING MEN

I read somewhere that, for Italians, all of life is a stage. They live their lives in public, strutting through the square on the evening *passeggio* simply to be seen. They have their arguments and marital breakdowns in the street too. That's why losing face is enough to drive a man to violent rage or suicide, and why Italian opera is so exaggerated. If it were not, it could never seem larger than the lives lived in every village square.

Malta wasn't like that at all. Maltese watchfulness was furtive. If I encountered a solitary walker in an alley near our house, he stared straight ahead—just like they do when driving—and passed me as though I wasn't there. But anytime I walked to the post office, the straggling line of old men who sat on the steps of the village church swiveled their heads in unison to follow my progress. If I glanced back, they quickly looked away. It was such a relief to go into the house and shut the door on the world.

Most of this staring tried to be covert, but the old lady across the street was different. She sat in her downstairs window all day, facing slightly sideways with an arm draped across the sill. Other old ladies stopped by for a chat and a few brought her groceries, but I never once saw her leave home. Her window was exactly opposite our front door, across a small open space, so our eyes met every time I stepped out. I never failed to wave and say hello, but my greetings were always met with a scowl. I wondered why she hated us.

I used to watch her sometimes from the balcony above our tall front door. I never saw anyone else on the other roofs, just one man who kept pigeons in a homemade coop. The Maltese only ascended to patch cracks after the first winter rains, or perhaps to hang laundry if they had a washroom. The village rooftops were a vision of flapping laundry: one day for sheets, one day for trousers, one day for intimate articles better left unexamined. We were the only ones who seemed to sit on our roof. Where we sought relief from the heat by taking our books up to read on wicker chairs beneath the olives, the Maltese dragged their furniture into the busy chattering streets.

We were renting the Palazzo Marija from Marian, whose father, Peter, bought the house when she was still a child. He told me it was once the summer home of an archbishop from Naples, and our living room had been his chapel. A later owner had cut a big hole in the wall facing the street and layered on thick coatings of bright yellow and marine-blue oil paint, turning the room into a garage. Chapel to garage—that's fitting, in a way, if you know anything about the reverence of an old Maltese man for his Sunday car.

Peter spent months on ladders carefully scraping away those thick layers of paint, lovingly revealing the natural stone beneath. Near the top of the walls, just below the ceiling arches, he had uncovered a series of flat plaster spaces that had once held frescoes. He thought they showed the story of Christ's crucifixion, the Stations of the Cross, but they had been obliterated by the hand that spread the paint, and no matter how carefully he attempted to uncover them he wasn't able to bring them back. All that remained was the clear fragment of a coat of arms in fresco on the capstone of an arch. I liked watching Peter work: the patience with which he mended a lock, or something as simple as a hinge, and his slow, considered manner of speech as he explained the abstract paintings he'd hung on the living room walls. He seemed to have absorbed something of the house's long, slow view of time.

An old Maltese house huddles around itself, turning its back on the street. There were signs of doorways that had been sealed off and traces of walls that had gone up and then come down. I sensed that the house had its own inner life, its own areas of memory that were sometimes walled off, perhaps because they were too painful to look at. The courtyard was a well of silence at its center, where sunlight filtered through the orange tree and lit the bursting bougainvillea that climbed the tower wall. It even lent a friendly shadow to dark stone steps that led to subterranean worlds in two separate cellars.

Whenever I looked at those walls, I saw the placid chips of Peter's restoration and how much care he'd put into it. When the light slanted in, the walls would begin to change. Limestone blocks that had been bleached white by harsh daytime sun were transformed into a rich honey color. If you were patient, like I was, you could watch it deepen.

Peter dropped by often in those early days to fix small things. When he was finished we would sit on wooden chairs in the kitchen and talk about his childhood during the war. "We lived in Birgu," he told me, "right next to the docks." Most of the population lived within six kilometers of the Grand Harbour, where the density was six times higher than the rest of the island. "The first air raid caught us by surprise. I remember the sirens going off and climbing down into rock-cut shelters in the ground with my parents."

He quickly learned to run for the nearest shelter when the siren sounded. Just sixty miles and five minutes' flying time from Axis airfields in Sicily, the Grand Harbour became one of the most heavily bombarded patches of rock in the world, suffering more than three thousand raids over a period of two years.

"It went on day after day," Peter said. "The earth shook, and we huddled together in the heat and the dark. We were so afraid." Bombs fell in such rapid succession that it created a continuous background roar. The ground shook so violently that, even in the rock-cut shelters, people stumbled and fell. "I hit my head against the wall in the darkness. I remember people were screaming, and I couldn't find my parents. Sometimes the entrance to a shelter would be blocked by rubble from falling buildings. Our shelters were connected from one house to the next, so we just came up somewhere else."

The island hadn't been equipped for a prolonged siege, but Malta was the only Allied base between Alexandria and Gibraltar, a vital point on Britain's lifeline to the Far East via the Suez Canal and India, and a strategic threat to Axis shipping routes in the struggle for North Africa. It couldn't be allowed to fall.

At first all they had were a few antiaircraft guns and three obsolete Gloucester Gladiator biplanes someone had found disassembled in storage. These were soon replaced by Hawker Hurricanes and Spitfires, but air crews were small, and with the island under tight blockade, spare parts, ammunition, and fuel were always in short supply.

In the face of impossible odds, military planners at the Lascaris war rooms, deep inside Valletta's massive stone bastions, devised a system of rotation that gave them around-the-clock fighter coverage and, eventually, the ability to intercept Axis bombers closer and closer to Italy. The operations center received information from six separate radar stations updated by radio every five minutes. They plotted aircraft positions by hand on an enormous map table and coordinated antiaircraft guns and fighter sorties across the island in real time. Enemy pilots who visited Malta as tourists after the war said they couldn't understand how "you always knew we were coming" or "how you had so many resources" despite the tight blockades. In reality, they had fewer than sixty aircraft, patched together with cannibalized parts, but somehow, despite the fatigue, the hunger, and the constant pressure, that brave group of men held off several thousand Nazi planes.

Bombs fell multiple times a day as Malta fought desperately to survive. Peter remembered one of the worst raids of March 1942. "There wasn't a single house left standing when we came out of the ground," he said. "It had all been destroyed." Homes collapsed, crushing their inhabitants. Straw mattresses burst into flames from the heat. Broken pipes trickled water into the dust of crushed stone. Electricity cables fell in tangled masses, and shattered glass filled the streets. Anyone caught in the open risked being torn apart by shrapnel. "So many people were buried alive. People walked dazed where streets used to be. And I saw carts piled with bodies."

The airfield at Ta' Qali had been hit by three hundred tons of bombs in forty-eight hours, dropped by some 220 enemy aircraft, and Mosta was struck repeatedly. "We were evacuated to Qormi soon after that," Peter said. "Many families were moved farther inland. We weren't bombed there—that was much better. But we were very hungry."

Agricultural production was inadequate in the best of times, capable of feeding just one-third of the population. With outside sources of food cut off, the island was on the brink of starvation. Food and water were running out. Rations for soldiers were reduced to two thousand calories a day. The island's livestock had been slaughtered long ago, and people used curtains to replace clothing and old automobile tires to resole their shoes. Disease had begun to spread too, due to poor sanitation and inadequate nutrition.

Peter told me about their suffering in such a matter-of-fact way, and then he stopped, lost in memory. "You know, people on Gozo had plenty to eat," he said. "They were far from the harbor and air-fields, and so they were never a target of the bombings. Their farms were untouched. But they refused to share their food with the rest of us, even as Malta starved. We've never forgotten it."

As war continued to rage across Europe, King George VI awarded the George Cross "to the island fortress of Malta—its people and defenders" on April 15, 1942. This highest civilian award for gal-lantry was followed by a U.S. Presidential Citation that read: "Under repeated fire from the skies, Malta stood alone and unafraid in the center of the sea, one tiny bright flame in the darkness—a beacon of hope for the clearer days which have come." The last raid took place in July 1943, and when the invasion of Italy began in September the fighting moved away.

"The war came to this house too," Peter said, and led me down stone stairs, pointing out two bomb shelters off the main cellar. One was shallow and had been closed decades before, but the other was open during his time of residence. The previous owners filled it with construction rubble, and when Peter took over the house he had the shelter sealed with stone. "They tell me it goes all the way to the cellar of the village church."

I could hear an echo from somewhere deep in the stone when he stomped on that corner of the floor. It was like a crack in the door to the underworld. If I held up a match, the flicker of strange breezes came through. Creatures—giant cockroaches and scorpions—crawled through into our world too, until I got a bucket of mortar and sealed the gaps.

# MELITA'S
# INFERNO

Summer in Malta came down like an affliction. The stagnant heat. The painful sun. Empty afternoon villages. Siestas where nothing moved and only the cicadas cried. But even in summer the marble floors of the house remained cool.

Every morning I opened the French doors to the courtyard to be greeted by the same heroic arc of blue sky. If clouds appeared, they were gossamer threads or unthreatening puffs that flitted across the firmament with an embarrassed air, as though they were unintended and didn't mean to cause offense.

The summer sky was only hazed when the wind shifted to the south, bringing the hot breath of Africa: the dreaded sirocco. It came from the south, across the Sahara, loading the air with sand and dust. The dry heat raised the temperature abruptly by several degrees, but moving air provided no relief. The sky would turn red and then brown. A haze would blot out the far side of the valley. Birds would fall silent. And then it would begin to rain mud. Warm, brown drops left yellow rivulets that streaked the walls and spattered white tiles. Vehicles were encrusted. Brown torrents ran down the streets, where they would normally run gray. The air was oppressive, and grit crunched between my teeth. The Maltese called it *xita tal-ħamrija*, "rain of soil." But then the sun would return, bringing more heat that dried the water and baked the mud to a firm crust. We knew it was over when the housewives emerged with their buckets and sponges. The front step would have to be polished again that day—preferably before Agnes down the block polished hers.

Once the heat had set in, government offices and many businesses closed at 1 p.m. and everyone fled to the beach. They called it summer hours and took it while earning full-time pay. I asked a Maltese friend how this worked. "We stay an extra hour every day in winter to make up for it," she said.

The afternoon air shimmered, and the stones of the houses were bleached white by the sun. Wooden shutters were kept firmly closed, to be opened again at night, but the chances of attracting cooler air were as faint as the nighttime breeze. On the worst of those days, we left off staring blankly at our desks and got in the car for the five-minute drive to the coast. As the villagers dozed in fitful sweat-soaked siestas, we swam at a rocky cove on the Delimara peninsula, where the sea rose and fell like the heartbeat of the world.

We sat on warm rock in a stony cove and ate thick sandwiches of crusty bread with tuna, capers, and sliced tomato pressed inside. Fruit picked fresh from a prickly pear left a slick of sticky juice on my chin, but it would be washed away by waves that were bracing in spring and later bathtub-warm. A shuffling digestive walk along broad limestone flats at the base of sea cliffs was always followed by another swim. The driver's seat of my car retained the damp print of wet shorts all season long, with sand on the floor mats and sunscreen streaks on the wheel.

We took our summer dinners at the wooden table in the courtyard because our little kitchen was far too hot. A plaster bust of Poseidon graced the wall behind me, as we sat beneath the orange tree eating baked fish drizzled with lemon, new potatoes, and squeaky green beans, washed down with a glass of wine the color of pale straw. The

orange tree cast moon shadows of dappled leaves on the tabletop and
on our plates. Ripe fruit dropped with a dull thud. Marble was wet
with dew. In the distance a dog barked, and then another.

The flat silver light of the moon lent the narrow twisting alleys a
glow that was entirely absent from the harsh shouting bustle of day. In
the stillness of the night it was easy to imagine an earlier Malta, from
the time of the Romans or the Phoenicians, when that small rock with
its hills gashed by dry valleys was a tiny speck in a vast mythological
sea. But it was only possible to maintain historical visions from inside
the walls of our house. Outside, after dark, those same village streets
felt huddled and forlorn, heavy with a legacy of old fears and resent-
ments. Something malevolent existed below the surface of life there.
It would take time to discover what that undertone meant.

"I was talking to a neighbor on my way back from the shop this morning," Tomoko said, stepping into the kitchen where I was hunched
over the cutting board making a sandwich. "I heard them speaking
Maltese, so instead of good morning I said bonjour. That's what everyone says." We'd been living in the village for two or three months,
and she was trying to pick up the language.

"What, the same as French?"

"Apparently not. Some old man said, 'No! We say bon-jew.' Like
that, with the emphasis on the first part. So I said, 'All right, then,' and
he corrected me again. 'Le le le,' he said, 'it's awwwwl-right.'"

"But that's just badly pronounced English..."

Maltese is the only Semitic language in the European Union and
the only Semitic language written using the Latin alphabet. To my
untutored ears, it combined the harshest noises of Arabic with the
most irritating bluster of Italian, with the result sounding like an
angry Sicilian who had spent too many years in the Maghreb. But
there was poetry within it.

The first written reference to a Maltese language (*lingwa maltensi*) comes from the will of a man called Paul Peregrino, dated 1436. Before that, the language had always been referred to as Arabic (*lingwa arabica*).

Maltese drifted away from Arabic over the centuries following the Norman reconquest of the islands, evolving independently of its mother tongue. According to linguist Joseph M. Brincat, the Maltese lexicon is composed of 32.4 percent words of Arabic origin, 55.5 percent of Italian origin (including Italian dialects), and 6.1 percent of English origin; however, "words derived from Arabic are more frequent because they denote the basic ideas and include the function words." So Maltese people still call god *Alla*. Lent, that forty-day period of self-imposed misery before Easter, is *Randan*, like the Arabic word *Ramadan*. And Easter itself is *L-Ghid*, which bears more than a passing resemblance to Eid, the Arabic word for feast.

Maltese remained the islanders' spoken language, with official documents being written first in Sicilian and then in Tuscan Italian, until it was displaced by English during the British centuries. A standard written orthography was only established in 1924, a project that took nearly two centuries.

To my newcomer's eyes, written Maltese seemed to have more silent letters than sounded ones: a blizzard of x's and j's and q's that were like a visual hedge maze without an exit, the sort that traps wanderers, sending them around in confusing circles until there's nothing left but bird-picked bones. Friends assured me they did have a sound, but I couldn't hear them. The name of our neighboring village was Ghaxaq, but I heard "asha." Mqabba wasn't "may-ba" at all, but "abba," like the Swedish pop group. And the posh seaside embassy district of Ta' Xbiex was pronounced "tash beesh," which has resulted in more misdirected taxis than any other place in the country.

The proficiency for swearing in the language was remarkable. Of course they had the standard phrases, such as *Busli sormi* (kiss my ass). But like Arabic, Maltese curses often referenced forcibly penetrating or otherwise degrading some member of the interlocutor's family. You might tell someone to *Busli l-bajd minn wara* (kiss my balls from behind), *F'ghoxx kemm ghandek* (fuck every person related to you or who you care about), or suggest *Ejja nahxu lil Anna f'sormha* (let's fuck Anna up the ass). But if you really wanted things to escalate quickly, you'd go with *Nahxilek L'ommok* (I'll fuck your mother), *F'ghoxx dik il-qahba ommok* (fuck your prostitute mother), or the extremely disturbing *F'ghoxx il-liba li xorbot ommok* (fuck the sperm your mother drank). Like Italians and Quebecois, Maltese also directed their wrath at the deity. Where Quebecois swear on the holy tabernacle, a Maltese might say *Haqq Alla* (fuck God) or *Haqq l-imbengla Madonna* (damn the bruised Virgin Mary).

But Maltese is not frozen in time. They also take foreign words like "constitution" and contort them into Maltese by swapping y for j. And so the national Center for Creativity became *Spazju Kreattiv*, Academy became *Akkademja*, and the local council became *kunsill lokali*. And don't even ask me for my *telefown, mowbajl*, or *imejl* contacts.

We went back out not long after Tomoko was corrected. I saw the cat lady sitting in her window and thought I'd try to greet her with the Maltese we'd just learned. I turned my face away for a moment and practiced working it into a smile, something confident and genuine, and then I turned back and said, "Bon-jew!" with great enthusiasm. I was watching her the whole time, and I don't know how else to describe it except to say that she receded very subtly. Her expression never changed; she just drifted backward as though she were on casters and slowly closed the shutter.

I was about to point this out to Tomoko when she stopped to examine a package that had been abandoned in the middle of the street.

She flipped it over with the toe of her shoe, stepped back, and said, "It's a cheese."

"What, a piece of cheese?"

"No, a wheel. Someone dropped an entire wheel of cheese and just left it here."

An old lady was coming down the alley at that moment. She stood next to my wife and contemplated the cheese. Then she prodded it with the tip of her shoe, turned to Tomoko, and shouted in her ear, "No good! No good. Don't eat that," and walked away.

# THE FEAST OF THE
# EXPLODING VILLAGE

We were woken one morning by a terrible wailing, a sound like a machine gone off its gears. As the initial shock wore off, I heard the insistent pounding of a drum grow closer and pass away.

"Do you hear a tuba?"

It was 8 a.m. on a Saturday, and a marching band was shuffling down the narrow street past our house. We would soon discover that our village had two marching bands: brass assemblies dressed like bus conductors, with lit cigarettes dangling from their lips or from the edge of a metal music stand. Months later I would formulate a theory that the marching band controlled the town. Little did I realize how true this was.

That afternoon I heard someone hammering outside my study. This was odd because I was one floor up. I opened the window and found myself face-to-face with a grizzled man in a flat cap. We were inches away from each other, but he just looked at me and kept talking to someone else on the ground. I couldn't think of how to break this awkward stare, so we gazed at each other until he was finished and I quietly closed the shutter. He had hammered a spike into the wall of our house and strung a wire with lights across the road. They were doing this all the way down the street.

A few days after these strange incidents I was startled from my bed by a massive bombardment of explosions. Civil war had just broken out in Libya, and two of their fighter jets had landed at our airport. At first I thought the conflict had spread across that small gap of sea and come directly to Zejtun, but it didn't sound like artillery. The patterns were too repetitive, and the source was quite near.

I pulled on my shorts and trudged up the steps of the tower to our highest roof. I could see the main church and the valley that separated our village from Tarxien. I watched for a few minutes and then trudged back down. "Fucking fireworks," I said.

"At eight in the morning?"

"Some idiots are setting off fireworks in the daytime."

Tomoko pointed at her ears and shook her head. We had to resort to the passing of notes.

As the bombardment increased, I expected windows to shatter at any moment and doors to leap off their hinges. A thin trickle of plaster dust was already falling from the ceiling as each new round threatened to bring down the walls around us. If Jericho could be felled by a trumpet, then surely this was enough to wipe all but a bunker off the map.

"Why would anyone do this to themselves?" I said, during a brief lull. No one was ever able to tell me. It was either an offering to the patron saint of hearing loss or an attempt at enacting the apocalypse.

We couldn't sleep, so we went to the gym. We returned to find all the streets to the village core blocked by police barricades. "I wonder if they've finally blown themselves off the face of the earth?" I said, rolling down my window. But apparently they were just getting started.

"Ground fireworks," the policeman said, as though this explained everything.

"But I live up there," I said, pointing down the main road.

"You can't go that way."

Someone laid on a horn behind me and edged up to my bumper. "We're new in town. How do I get over there? Triq Santa Marija is one-way."

He pointed at the other side of the village, shrugged, and walked away.

I turned down the nearest street and was swept up in a maze of alleys that ran in a series of concentric circles. Because the village core was blocked, even more people than usual were driving down the alleys the wrong way. Maltese drivers never creep; they hurtle maniacally. Meeting in the middle involved both vehicles coming to a screeching stop. The drivers would sit and stare at each other, waiting for the other person to break the stalemate by reversing erratically to a wider place. If too much time passed and no one gave in, there would be shouting and swearing and threats.

This was our introduction to the village feast.

The *festa* is the main event of the Maltese summer. Every village has at least one, but normally two, because Maltese life is a dichotomy: two feasts, two marching bands, two political parties. There was something Zoroastrian about it. To the uninitiated, every festa looked exactly the same, but "feast junkies" traveled from village to village all summer long to attend them. Even if you weren't an enthusiast, this week, culminating on the weekend with the saint's procession, was unmissable.

Old ladies had been knocking on doors for months, collecting donations that I thought went to the decorations and statues but were probably spent mostly on petards, or *murtali*—those enormous, monotonous aerial bombs. Volunteers polished the interior of the church to a rich brassy shine, repainted statues and wooden posts for the main streets, and gave a good dusting to embroidered banners—the *pavaljuni*—that turned every alley into a magical aisle of red and gold. Residents erected flags on the roof of every house too, so many that the entire village bristled like an enraged porcupine.

The week of the feast was marked by constant bombardments of petards from morning to night. Each evening the alley in front of our house filled with the sound of shuffling feet as the entire population of the village funneled past. Our neighbors had placed small candles in paper bags outside their doors, casting a warm glow and causing shadows to flicker on the walls.

It took half an hour to make our way from the corner of our street to the *pjazza*. The crowds were so thick that we were reduced to the sort of slow shuffle that brings static electricity out of thick carpets. My height made navigating easier, but I was cut off at the knee by a baby's pram, and the shoulders of my shirt glowed with a fine dusting of face powder, as though I'd been handling moths.

Maltese are not quiet people, and in a large group, with so many conversations happening at once, we had to shout over the background roar.

"It looks like a garbage truck exploded," I said. Perhaps an errant petard had set one off?

A crumpled fast food bag spotted with grease tumbled past, and streamers and chunks of burned paper swirled like snow. Three empty beer bottles had been set into the potted plants by someone's door, next to a crumpled cigarette package wedged into the bars of a window. I was about to point this out, but I was drowned out by a marching band as it took up a tune: "Thump thump thump. Thump thump thump." Then the wailing horns kicked in.

The heat and the noise and the firework fumes were doing something strange to my head. By the time we reached the entrance of the church, which was covered in strings of brilliant white lightbulbs, the lines of reality had begun to blur. The doors smoked like the mouth of hell, belching great clouds of frankincense, with a bottleneck of sinners pushing to get in. Inside the church the clouds cleared slowly, flickering with the hazy light of hundreds of candles, polished marble, gleaming wooden pews, a brilliance of lace, and the dim chiaroscuro of oil paintings. We slipped down a stairway into the crypt, where I was hoping to find traces of a bomb shelter or a tunnel that might have led to our cellar, but the crowds were thick down there too, and the heavy air made it difficult to breathe.

Back outside, I bought two cans of beer from a vendor and stood aside to survey the scene.

"What now?" Tomoko spoke to an old man next to her. It took a few attempts to find someone who understood English.

"He said the marching band will play." The man shouted something else in her ear. "Tonight it's Beland Band Club. Tomorrow night the other band will try to compete and outdo them."

You had to pick a side. The man said that if you lived in our part of town, you wore red and supported the Zejtun Band Club. If you lived a few houses away, beyond the street that led to the church, you wore green and supported Beland. You should cheer loudly on the nights when your own band plays and shout insults at supporters of the other band, or at the façade of their band club. When their night comes you must stand mute and angry, unimpressed by their playing and oblivious to their insults. This is driven by *pika*, a form of no-holds-barred rivalry characterized by hostility, ill-feeling, and jealousy. The village bands compete against each other, and the village of Zejtun competes with neighboring villages like Tarxien, Paola, or Għaxaq to see who has the loudest feast. They are aided by the local artillery: each band club also has its own fireworks factory.

Hidden down laneways on the outskirts of villages, the fireworks factories of the marching band clubs squatted in the middle of farmers' fields where, behind thick stone walls, amateur enthusiasts taught each other to make aerial bombs. These structures exploded with great regularity, often killing several members of the same family, who were then declared to be martyrs slain while serving the village's patron saint. In Malta the ability to make farting sounds with a tuba also qualified one to handle large quantities of TNT.

"So what happens next?" I said.

"It seems like they're getting ready for something," Tomoko replied.

We took up a place near the wall of the church, where we could watch the scene without feeling like a bumper in a pinball machine. A heavy smell of rancid grease filled the air. The pjazza was surrounded by fast food trucks ringed like a circle of wagons, dispensing fried chicken, french fries, and enormous hamburgers. Everyone seemed to be eating frantically.

"Let's go look for traditional foods," Tomoko shouted. Food stalls are a big part of Japanese festivals, where there's always something different to try, something regional alongside typical festival foods, but all we could find in Zejtun was a deserted nougat stall. We bought a stick out of curiosity. It was comically overpriced, tasted like sawdust, and chipped three of my teeth.

"That old man told me Saturday is the big night," Tomoko said, with hands cupped around my ear. "They bring out the statue of the saint for a procession around the church and let off the largest fireworks display. And then there's another religious procession on Sunday morning, but that one is quieter."

I knew the morning procession would be made up of old people, a shuffling geriatric ward of the devout. Given the scale of the weeklong street party, everyone else would be hung over, or in hospital with perforated eardrums.

People were standing around chatting as midnight approached. Beer was consumed in industrial quantities, bells clanged maniacally, and the marching band played a few cacophonous songs. There was a feeling of anticipation in the air. We waited. And waited. And waited some more. But we finally gave up and fought our way back to our street. Nothing had happened at all.

The feast continued with daily bombardments that shook chunks of stone loose from the walls and drove every attempt at work from my head. We went back to the pjazza for one more evening, but nothing happened that night either, apart from the roar of conversation and music played from several directions at once. And that's when I figured it out.

"Nothing's supposed to happen," I said.

Tomoko looked puzzled—understandably so.

"The petard enthusiasts try their best to blow up the town. The marching band farts out a few tunes, the same ones they muddle through every year. And everyone stands in the square eating fast food and talking to the same people they've seen every day for the last thirty years. But they dress up a little when they do it."

"And?"

"That's it. Trust me, I'm from a four-thousand-person town. I've lived a version of this before—without the explosions."

I looked around for a rubbish bin and placed my empty beer bottle in it. I still couldn't bring myself to leave it on a window ledge or in someone's flower pot.

When sanity finally descended on Zejtun, the ensuing feast started in the next village over. It began with a morning bombardment of petards, and because it was just across the field it was nearly as loud as the one in our town.

Malta in summer was a lot like living in the middle of a firing range, but despite their explosive omnipresence, I never met a Maltese person who admitted to liking petards. Only someone with an incredible tolerance for the repetitive could possibly take any delight in it. As the season wore on, I found myself wondering if I dug a deep enough shelter, would I be able to form a coherent thought or read a paragraph all the way through? But sadly, no. Tunneling would just be busywork and a distraction. Earplugs held no power over the petard, nor did any form of industrial hearing protection. Nothing short of total deafness—and even then you'd still feel the explosions resonating in your chest.

A residue of thick, toxic smoke filled our valley and fell on the fields below, and much was washed into the sea, along with the partially burned paper that fluttered down from the sky. Fireworks chemicals were also measured in the food chain in significant amounts. At least one of the chemicals used in these bombs was banned in Europe as a likely carcinogen.

We would be blindsided by these insistent, repetitive, indefatigable bombardments on every national, local, or invented holiday, but I never suffered the main village festa again. I marked it on the calendar and booked a trip abroad. The only way to escape the noise was to leave the island and go as far away as possible, say, to Murmansk or Tristan da Cunha.

I asked a friend's teenage daughter about this strange obsession with backyard explosives. She said, "Yes, well…that is a hobby of the uneducated."

The way she said "uneducated"—choosing her words so carefully—made me suspect she was avoiding a more common term, one with loaded connotations. It was my first glimpse into the major class division of Maltese society: *hamalli* versus *tal-pepe*.

A local satirical publication said that *tal-pepe* traditionally came from villages like Sliema, Saint Julian's, and Attard. Staunch supporters of the Nationalist Party, they were known for hanging out in what they thought were the fashionable places of the moment, dressed in the latest styles, with enormous sunglasses. They spoke their own

version of English, which they believed sounded posh—"Well, I was
up to Lon-don last week, and we went to Ox-ford"—and often didn't
speak Maltese at all.

The Maltese-English dictionary gave the meaning of *hamallu* (sin-
gular of *hamalli*) as "low class or vulgar." It included anyone whose behavior was crude: lager louts, violent bullies, or obnoxious show-offs
obsessed with team sports and flashy cars. But historically, *hamalli*
was also an offensive term applied to people from working-class back-
grounds, and it had geographical connotations.

*Hamalli* were said to be from the south, villages like Qrendi,
Zejtun, and Zurrieq. They often spoke only Maltese, dropped out
of school at age fifteen, and tended to support the Labour Party.
According to a Maltese blog, "They're generally happy with their
simplistic way of life and will shower you with affection if they take
a liking to you—just don't commit the cardinal sin of insulting their
mother. Then they'll get all their cousins and friends to hunt you
down and kill you."

My friends were drawn from both sides. Each group looked down
on the other, one as illiterate uncultured morons and the other as
phony effeminate snobs. As with all stereotypes, there was an element
of truth and an element of exaggeration to each. But this divide went
much deeper than Labour versus Nationalist or south versus north.
It seemed to describe two very different cultures inhabiting the same
claustrophobic space.

# GENTLEMAN
# PIRATES

Our distant village was far from the café-crowded expat centers. We had Sammy's takeaway kiosk that did pizza on weekends, and that was all. Dinner in the tiny capital of Valletta was the highlight of our social calendar.

"I'm hungry enough to eat a horse," I said, taking up a menu on a warm June night.

"We have that," the waiter replied, cutting in. "And to drink?"

"Two Campari and sodas to start. And a small plate of snails."

The bitter stimulus of Campari formed the perfect opening to any Mediterranean meal because it contained sunshine as well as sustenance. The snails had been plucked by hand from the stones of the garigue. The capers that covered our fish grew locally, too, on the sides of the massive defensive bastions that ring the Grand Harbour.

My horse arrived: grilled and tender, with a strong tang of iron. "You know that's an aphrodisiac," I said, filling Tomoko's glass with a crisp, cold pinot grigio. "You'd better watch out."

She just rolled her eyes, squeezing a wedge of lemon over delicate slices of carpaccio as the waiter brought baked grouper sprinkled with capers. The setting was completed with a large bowl of potatoes smothered in olive oil, grilled vegetables, and a small dish of firm black olives.

Our conversation was interrupted by a parade of new arrivals who burst in with the sort of shouting that's designed to attract attention. It was their night on the town, and they wanted everyone to know it. The men wore black suits, gold chains, and trousers so tight I wondered how they managed to slip a credit card into a pocket. Pink shirts and baby blues completed the look. Women dressed in the tightest and shortest of skirts, tottering around on stiletto heels with all the risk and none of the grace of a circus performer. A Maltese friend who'd written for fashion magazines gave a comically scathing opinion of the local aesthetics.

"They stuff themselves into a Lebanese-style sequined dress with thick makeup," she said, "caking it on to the point where they look like someone's fruity divorced mother trying to pick up the lads. God, that Maltese taste…"

"But why?" I said. "Where does it come from?"

"They think women should look like that to be *faqa* and *sexy hee* and *bomba* and *bay-yoo-tiful inside and out*. This so-called bombastic is the trailer-trash idea of dressing up. The irony is that the older a woman gets, the more aging all this caked-on makeup, overstyled hair, and skimpy clothes becomes." She shrugged. "They end up looking like a guest at a Lebanese wedding crossed with an Italian porn star on a night out."

In the villages where we lived our island lives, T-shirts and faded shorts were the norm at the local takeaway. The "posh" towns and rural villages felt very far apart.

The menu was brought again when the commotion of arrival had died down, but desserts in Malta were always the same and we had already grown tired of them. Panna cotta. Banoffee pie. Ice cream.

"What do you have?" I'd ask. And they would say, "We have va-nil-la and choc-o-late."

We skipped dessert in favor of a walk down to Saint Barbara's Bastions. The late-night streets were empty; only parked cars and stray cats lined the road. Across the Grand Harbour in Birgu, super-yachts basked in their own reflection below Fort Saint Angelo, and wooden fishing boats and sailboats bobbed in oily harbor water.

I will always remember my first view of that harbor. We had just concluded day one of house hunting. Neither of us was feeling very optimistic after eight hours spent on congested roads that connected even more congested towns. The rental agent said, "I have to go home now, but do you want me to drop you off in Valletta? It's still early."

She left us near the Phoenicia hotel, just beyond the old city gates. As we pushed past the crowds and entered Republic Street, the history of this small island spread out before us and I completely forgot the ugliness of Paceville's nightclub district with its hideous urban sprawl. When we stepped onto the heights of the Upper Barrakka Gardens and saw the Grand Harbour, I was stopped in my tracks by one of the most impressive views in the entire Mediterranean.

The area had been used as a harbor since Phoenician times, but the Middle Ages had given it a bewildering series of honey-colored bastions, demi-bastions, curtains, and ravelins that rose more than a hundred meters from the murky dockside waters. Fort Saint Elmo and the now dilapidated Fort Ricasoli guarded the Grand Harbour's mouth, with Fort Saint Angelo on a peninsula opposite the high garden where we stood. The other side of Valletta, and the harbor of Marsamxett, was covered by the battery at Tigne Point and by Fort Manoel on Manoel Island.

A profusion of anchorages and dockyard facilities had been established in the main creeks around the great basin's fringes: Rinella

Creek, Kalkara Creek, Dockyard Creek, and French Creek. Commercial shipping moved to the free port at Kalafrana, and dockyard business dried up when the British navy pulled out, but that traffic—and revenue—has been replaced by a steady flow of cruise ships from across the Mediterranean.

The knights in shining armor who built this architectural jewel had been reluctant immigrants. The Order of Knights of the Hospital of Saint John of Jerusalem, or the Knights Hospitaller, was a militarized religious group that arose in the eleventh century to provide care for sick, poor, or injured pilgrims going to the Holy Land. From the time of the First Crusade, they were also tasked with defending the Holy Land against Islamic forces. Initially fairly successful, they established fortifications on the mainland and later on the island of Rhodes, but the tide eventually turned and they were defeated by Suleiman I after a prolonged siege and driven out of the Levant in 1522.

The now homeless knights bounced around Europe for the next seven years, presumably sleeping on park benches and begging various rulers to grant them a place where they could settle to continue their work. They were offered Tripoli in 1530 by the king of Sicily, Holy Roman Emperor Charles V, provided that they would also take Malta. The delegation they sent to examine the archipelago returned with tales of a waterless, poverty-stricken place, barren of resources, with a troublesome population. They said, "Thanks, but we'll keep looking." Unfortunately, no one else was willing to cede them territory, so Malta it would be. They'd have to make the best of it.

The island already had an administrative center at Mdina, established by the Romans but fortified by Arabs who conquered the tiny archipelago in 870 CE as Islam swept North Africa and crossed to Sicily. These new colonists had introduced crops like citrus fruits and cotton, irrigated by waterwheels, and delicacies that still form the heart of Maltese cookery: almonds, figs, spices, and sweet pastries. They left their mark on the language too, with place-names, family names, and even a style of singing bearing unmistakably Arab origins. Their hegemony would last more than two hundred years, until the Normans drove them out early in the twelfth century, ushering in several centuries of absentee rule by a series of feudal lords, barons, and crowned heads of Europe.

Now the islands were changing hands again. Malta's new owners ignored Mdina. The knights were a seafaring power, and they chose instead to occupy an existing fortification at what is now Fort Saint Angelo, to enlarge it and make the Grand Harbour their base, a position it would hold for 268 years. They left internal matters largely in the hands of the existing structures. It really didn't seem like they wanted to be bothered with it.

They weren't given much time to settle in. A series of pirate raids by the corsair Dragut prompted the knights to strengthen Fort Saint Angelo and to build a new structure, Fort Saint Elmo, at the end of the Sciberras peninsula by the harbor's mouth. They managed to do it all in six months. But these defenses would barely be adequate to fight off the invasion everyone expected would come.

After several years of ominous rumors, the Ottoman navy finally arrived on May 18, 1565, determined to take the island back for Islam and wipe out the Knights of Saint John—now the Knights of Malta—once and for all. When the Turkish armada set sail from Istanbul, it was the largest assembled since ancient times: some 193 vessels carrying approximately 48,000 invaders. The Knights could draw on 6,000 men, nearly half of which were soldiers called up from the local Maltese population. Hopeless odds, but the seeds of division were already present in the invading forces.

The Ottoman command had been split three ways, between the leader of the land forces, Piyale Pasha, and the supreme naval commander, Mustafa Pasha, who both deferred to the corsair Dragut when he arrived from Tripoli. After much argument, the fleet decided to anchor in Marsamxett Bay rather than attack Fort Saint Angelo by land, a tactic that would very likely have succeeded. But to berth their ships in Marsamxett they would first have to take tiny Fort Saint Angelo. That decision would prove their undoing.

The Turks dragged their powerful guns to the high ground of the Sciberras peninsula, from which they expected to reduce Saint Elmo to rubble in a matter of days. They did manage to flatten much of the fort, but the Knights evacuated the wounded under cover of darkness and resupplied the fort from across the harbor. They fought to the last man, selling their lives to buy precious time for the promised reinforcements from Sicily. The siege also cost the Ottomans their finest commander. Dragut was killed by friendly fire when a cannon exploded and sent shards from its own parapet in all directions. Saint Elmo held out for twenty-eight days.

When Mustafa finally stormed the fort and put the badly wounded survivors to the sword, he had the bodies of the knights decapitated and floated across to Fort Saint Angelo on wooden crucifixes. In response, Grand Master Jean Parisot de Valette decapitated all the Turkish prisoners held by the knights, stuffed their bloody heads into his cannons, and fired them into the Turkish camp. This would be a fight to the end.

The Turks now turned their attention—and their guns—fully onto the Senglea peninsula and Fort Saint Angelo. The walls were pounded with cannon by day and rebuilt by the defenders each night, and assaults were launched from land and sea. De Valette himself rushed to the scene of the worst fighting, time and again, with sword in hand, boosting the determination of all who saw him. Defeat was narrowly avoided more times than anyone could count, but the knights and the Maltese held out until the weather turned at the start of September.

Ottoman morale was deteriorating badly. This should have been an easy prize, given their numerical superiority and their command of the high ground. As the summer wore on, brutal heat caused illness to spread through the Turkish camp, established on low marshy ground at the Marsa end of the harbor. If they didn't leave soon, the seasonal Mediterranean storms would begin, forcing them to winter on Malta. They were already packing their camp when the long-promised relief force finally arrived from Spain and landed some 8,000 men at Saint Paul's Bay. The newcomers got there just in time to massacre a few retreating Turks.

Malta survived, and Europe was safe from the specter of invading Islamic hordes. The Ottomans had lost some ten thousand regular forces, plus volunteers and pirates. The knights were reduced by one-third, and Malta lost around a third of its population. Fortifications and dwellings on the Senglea peninsula and Birgu were flattened. But they had held off the might of the Ottoman Empire for more than four months in what would go down in history as the last epic battle of Crusader Knights.

The Great Siege of 1565 left the Hospitallers feeling vulnerable in their poorly defended fort in the middle of Birgu. They were overlooked on two sides: by the Corradino heights to the south, and by the spine of the waterless Sciberras peninsula across the Grand Harbour, the same rocky spine the Turks had used to flatten Fort Saint Elmo. The conflict had taught them that to be secure in Malta, they must turn the Sciberras peninsula into a fortress.

They began a great campaign of building on those heights, culminating in the city of Valletta, their crown jewel, "built by gentlemen for gentlemen," with its soaring bastions, sheltered harbor, and late-Baroque palaces. The orderly grid-plan streets made it possible to stand near City Gate and look all the way down the urban limestone canyon of Republic Street to the sea at the town's distant Saint Elmo end.

Valletta had the splendid assurance of a strong place that is also a beautiful one. Members were required to bequeath their wealth to the order when they died, and given that most knights were nobles with vast holdings in continental Europe, they were soon brimming with cash. They embellished their city with fortifications, churches, palaces, and works of art, and for about a century this small corner of Malta was a truly magnificent place.

They continued to run their famous hospital, with a standard of hygiene and care far in advance of anything to be found elsewhere in Europe, but as the Muslim armies stopped pushing their way into Europe, the Knights of Malta gradually lost their sense of purpose. By the 1640s their crusading spirit had faded. Where they once confined their attacks to Muslim shipping, now they were also attacking Venetian and other Christian ships on the flimsiest of pretexts, stealing from their allies when it suited them. The once great knights had drifted into common piracy.

Privateering was practiced in Malta before the knights' arrival, but the metal-clad Holy Crusaders boosted the trade by giving it their blessing and in turn took a tax cut from a dubious activity on the fringes of legality. It soon became one of the main commercial activities on the islands. Most of the profits came from kidnapping—stealing and trafficking human slaves—while the rest came from cargo and from precious material like gold and spices. But the benefits weren't confined to those who sailed the ships or manned a cannon. Historian Liam Gauci writes that regular Maltese citizens put money into these ventures, backing a ship for a share of the take. Even the nuns who prayed for the success of a ship got a legal 5 percent cut.

Malta would become one of the most important corsairing centers in the Mediterranean, with a reputation for having the best dockyard, the best technology, the latest weapons, and some of the most highly skilled pirate crews between Europe and Algeria. The island was also a ready market for the spoils of war, taking on the role of a fence that disposes of stolen goods. Foreigners moved to the island to get a corsair license in the same way offshore companies set up there today to practice their own brand of legal piracy.

Malta's corsairing activities were finally stopped by the British in the 1820s, and that ingrained drive for easy money took a different turn. As Britain poured cash into the Grand Harbour's dockyards, transforming them into a naval base, a narrow Valletta alley called Strait Street developed into one of the island's many hubs of vice. Noisy sailor bars lined the alley, which seamen called the "Gut," and the entire harbor teemed with brothels offering prostitutes of all ages and both genders. Men pimped their wives, mothers prostituted their children, and fathers rented their underage sons to sailors for cash. Sex workers were murdered, and children were routinely raped for money. Maltese emigrants also took those skills abroad. Starting in the 1930s, prostitution in London's Soho district was controlled by Maltese gangsters, until tougher Albanian gangs pushed them out at the beginning of the twenty-first century. Gentlemen's clubs are still a prominent feature of Paceville, Malta's current nightclub district.

During our time on the island, European investigative journalists would reveal how the tiny country operated as a sort of virtual pirate base for tax avoidance within the European Union, to the detriment of their fellow member states. Online gaming companies flocked to Malta for its lax regulatory controls and easy banking, a situation that was exploited by Italian mafia families to launder funds. The government peddled golden residency schemes and sold Maltese (European Union) citizenship under its Individual Investor Program, providing oligarchs from Russia, China, and the Arab states with the ability to live anywhere in the twenty-seven countries of the EU's Schengen Area. The government also tried to lure cryptocurrency operators with a marketing scheme centered on "blockchain island," but it failed when banks refused to open accounts for a high-risk enterprise that few financial institutions seemed to understand.

Fuel was smuggled from Libya, too, and transshipped on the edge of Maltese territorial waters while the island's authorities turned a blind eye. Tuna was laundered for multimillion euro profits. A Chinese-run factory operated with North Korean slave labor. And tobacco and drugs passed through on locally flagged ships. If there was a scam that could be thought up, chances are it found its way to Malta, where someone was always willing to get involved for a cut.

# TWO

# STRANGE

# CRIMES

# HELL
# ON WHEELS

As our first island summer raged on, politics raged too. The nation was in the midst of a divorce referendum, and politicians and the Catholic clergy were fighting hard to split things down the middle.

The church once had great power in Malta. Travel writer Paul Theroux, after a brief visit, described the island as "low, almost tree-less, dusty, hot, and priest-ridden," presumably in reference to a period when Malta's feudal theocracy exercised control through illiteracy, coercion, and fear of the Inquisition—at least until the brief two-year French occupation (1798–1800) when Napoleon tried to break the church's power. The Labour prime minister, Dom Mintoff, did the rest, forcing through a separation of church and state beginning in 1971.

At first I assumed the Maltese were a deeply pious people, given the astonishing number of churches on the island: apparently 365 of them, one for every day of the year. But when self-interest came into conflict with moral duty, Jesus was quickly set aside. Divorce had always been illegal on the island, but most of the people I met had been separated at least once, sometimes twice. Those who could afford it traveled abroad for their divorce, and it would be quietly recognized back home. Abortions were said to be carried out in the same discreet way. But these privileges were the realm of the lucky few.

The *Times of Malta* wrote that by 1994 the number of separations amounted to 60 percent of the number of new marriages. Families collapsed in high dramas of infidelity, drawing in relatives and friends who relished nothing more than a good village argument. Each partner then went off and started a new family with someone else, a child or two quickly arrived, and so on, geometrically, algorithmically, complicating each family tree with a tangled mess of half-brothers and -sisters, stepparents, quarter-cousins, illegitimate kids, and hyphenated names. Inheritance often resulted in nasty feuds.

All this was about to change during the government of Prime Minister Lawrence Gonzi (2004–13), thanks to a private member's bill in parliament. As nations around the world debated same-sex marriage and equal rights for homosexual families, the people of Malta were grappling with an issue 90 percent of the world took for granted, and only two other countries—the Philippines and Vatican City— deemed illegal. It was almost as though they were considering giving women the vote.

The church issued a pastoral letter on the Sunday before referendum day, encouraging parishioners to vote no on May 28, 2011, which prompted complaints of religious pressure. Roadside billboards asked passing motorists, "What would Jesus think?" and the *Times of Malta* was filled with letters to the editor, like one by Joe Zammit from Paola, titled "Hell is real and eternal." After working himself into an ecclesiastical fury, Zammit closed his letter with the words, "I pray earnestly and often to the Holy Trinity for the dying who are still in mortal sin and are on the precipice of eternal damnation." When the vote finally came, the proposal was approved by 53 percent of the population.

The fight over divorce had briefly torn the island apart, but strong emotions didn't last long in the Mediterranean. Religious anger was soon replaced by hope. The buses were on the way.

The tourist shops of Malta peddled plastic knights, ornaments made from Mdina glass, tinned olives and capers, and those round blue amulets you see everywhere in the Levant that promise protection from the evil eye, but one of the most popular items on offer was the die-cast public buses. The public transportation system of Malta was so old that it had become a tourist attraction.

The British brought Bedford buses to the island during colonial times, and when we arrived in 2011 those vehicles were still in service. Each bus was the property of the individual driver, though they had formed some sort of organized confederacy that licensed and regulated their routes. They were painted canary yellow, with pithy slogans in script across the windshield—"Heaven in Hell", for example, or "Sex Machine"—and the inside near the driver's cabin was encrusted with such an abundance of religious iconography that they bordered on portable altars. Of course, most drivers didn't lavish such attention on unseen areas like the exhaust system or the engine, so those quaint lacquered buses hurtled down the island's potholed roads trailing great clouds of black smoke and breaking down with stubborn regularity.

British tourists still came to Malta to photograph the buses, reliving their wartime childhoods with imperial red public telephone booths and bad food, but only the British and the bus drivers themselves lamented their passing, lumping these outdated vehicles with other "quaint" island habits like the noise and the petards and the terrible driving. It was one thing to take a token bus ride from Valletta or Sliema to Mdina—"What a great story to tell Aunt Marge!"—but it was another thing entirely to rely on a bus from the 1950s for your daily commute.

Leather seats were worn down by generations of sweaty backsides; the metal frames showed through; and the shock absorbers had been destroyed long ago by the island's horrid roads. The buses gave a taste of eternal hellfire in summer, when the sun raised the temperature of anything metal to that of a branding iron. When the winter rains came, the humidity and the funk of damp wool made riding one feel like being inside a musty humidifier. At least you could always rely on the driver to verbally abuse you. Drivers shortchanged customers with great regularity, especially foreigners, raking in an extra penny or two on each fare for that cunning retirement plan. You were sure to be cursed at in Maltese, and your questions sneered at, and you would never be let out where the bus promised to stop, near that tourist attraction you weren't sure how to find.

But all this was about to end. During the summer of our arrival, the island was teetering on the brink of modernity. The government had purchased a fleet of new modern, air-conditioned buses, and they were on the way. Awl-right, *mela*, they were used buses, and they'd bought them from China, but public transportation on the island would step from the 1950s to the early 2000s in a single time-machine leap.

Shaking hands fluttered newspapers with anticipation as each new development trickled out. The buses were being loaded onto ships in China. And then the buses were on their way. The arrival of the buses was imminent. Stay tuned, people, stay tuned. And then…yes…they were here. The archbishop was photographed blessing the buses, and on Monday everyday life would be transformed as the fleet rolled out proudly in their uniform blue-and-white paint jobs, replacing the old.

That's when things started to go wrong. The franchise had been contracted to Arriva, a foreign firm that successfully managed bus and rail services in fourteen European Union countries. They took it for granted that they would bring their new island service up to a modern standard and that everyone would love them for it. But they should have sent an anthropologist, because Arriva had gravely misunderstood the Maltese.

I'd seen the occasional bus tootling around the island in recent weeks as trainee drivers wandered the roads, learning routes and being instructed by foreign teachers. The company had already caused some controversy when they refused to hire the old bus drivers en masse. These guys clearly expected to transition to the new company with all the same perks and a higher rate of pay, but Arriva saw how few of them were up to its standards. Their refusal to take them on anyway was a knife in the back of the Maltese patronage network. When the big day arrived and the new service was set to begin, half the drivers didn't show up for work. Total chaos on day one didn't bode well, but it was just the beginning.

The problem can be summarized in a few brief sentences. The streets of Maltese villages are very small; most are narrow alleys that twist and turn with medieval irregularity. The King Long buses, as their name suggests, were very large; many were even extended bendy buses. They simply didn't fit.

The newspapers soon filled with stories of buses that found themselves wedged between buildings. I say "found themselves wedged" because no one seemed to understand how they got there. It was always reported in the passive tense, as something that happened rather than something that was caused. Each new humiliation was worse than the one before. One driver didn't know his own route, so he took directions from a passenger, and when the street grew smaller and smaller and he'd passed the point of being able to turn around, rather than admit his error he plunged forward until his bus was firmly stuck.

Empty buses rolled down hills and smashed into walls when drivers forgot to set the brake. One furious reader sent a video to the *Times of Malta* showing a driver who attempted to squeeze his King

Long between a wall and a car parked illegally on a double yellow line. He didn't quite make it, of course, but when metal began to scrape against metal, he was unable to admit his error. We see him on the video hesitating for just a moment, but rather than lose face, he stepped on the gas. Pedestrians yelled and threw up their arms. Passengers screamed "Madonna!" The street was filled with the sound of grinding metal as bus dragged car half a block down the road before finally breaking free and speeding off.

I read the paper avidly for each new incident and diligently cut out the articles, but they happened with such regularity that I eventually lost interest and abandoned my clipping file. The entire thing was just so predictable. In less than two years those shiny new buses looked like they'd been worked over by secret police. They were filthy and dented. The engines howled in protest when they struggled up a hill. The air-conditioning—a major selling point to the public—had stopped working on most of them. And all the buses were soon trailing great clouds of black smoke as though they were powered by coal. Then they began to catch fire. Sometimes it happened while they idled unattended in a yard, and sometimes it happened when passengers were onboard. The unmaintained engines simply burst into flames. The Maltese were quick to blame the other political party, the Chinese, and the foreign bus company, but they never pointed the finger at themselves.

Like Russians after the fall of the USSR, bus commuters pined for the old system. Arriva couldn't get the schedule right because traffic on the island was growing worse by the day, and the drivers wouldn't cooperate. Rather than come together to find a solution, the government refused to take any heat or to make tough decisions with the pampered unions and obstructing officials. To cite an apt cliché, they immediately and unhesitatingly threw Arriva under the bus, blaming every problem on them. The company brought in foreign drivers—professionals trained under normal professional standards—to try to force Malta into the modern world, but even that was to no avail. Arriva finally left the island in defeat early in 2014. They threw up their hands in frustration, canceled the ten-year contract, and walked away after just three years.

The Labour Party was in power by then, and they were quick to take advantage of the situation. A mismatched fleet of new "chartered" buses soon took to the road. Most were tourist coaches, proudly operated by party supporters who were charging the government a reported €13,000 per month per bus—plus frequent overtime—to operate these same routes. Some of the old Arriva buses were hauled into service too. Those that were still drivable had the Arriva logo obscured with a thin slash of white paint. The months and the spiraling deficits piled up, but the free-for-all couldn't last forever. The government eventually found another foreign company to take over. New buses were purchased, again with European Union funds, and many of the same problems began to recur.

"What were they thinking?" I said, reading about the latest cronyism in the newspaper.

"Who?" Tomoko said, looking up from her coffee.

"This Spanish company. Why wouldn't they just call up Arriva and say, 'How come you left Malta?' I'm sure they'd give them an earful. No one in their right mind would try to do business here. Mark my words. It will end in disaster."

The former CEO of Arriva, David Martin, did eventually speak out in 2016, admitting that, in hindsight, Arriva's move to Malta was doomed to fail. "We struggled to maintain anything to do with sensible driving standards," he said. "Our accident rates were unbelievable; the quality of drivers there was incredibly bad."

When I told a local friend I'd bought a car, he said, "Got insurance? You'll need it."

Maltese weren't kidding when they said, "We don't drive on the left or the right, we drive in the shade."

"No one uses a turn signal," my friend continued. "And if they do, they're just as likely to turn in the opposite direction from the one you're expecting. The hazard light serves as a parking permit for anyone who wants to block the road to buy a *pastizzi*, triple-park in front of a garage, or stop in a narrow lane to have a nice long chat."

"What should I do in a situation like that? Just lay on the horn?"

"I suggest you bring a book."

Maruti four-wheel-drive Gypsies with prehensile arms dangling from a window careened down roads more potholed than a field after the Third Battle of Ypres. At times it was like hurtling down a fume-clogged drainage embankment. The drivers of ancient trucks overloaded with limestone blocks rolled straight into main roads with no regard for oncoming traffic. Cars came at us in the wrong lane, usually around blind corners. Head-on collisions were common; I had never seen so many. But most perplexing of all were the single-car accidents. The newspapers reported several each week. A car would suddenly fly off a perfectly straight road and plow into a stone wall or a tree, or do a barrel roll down the center line. I'd read about it in the paper next day: "Single-car accident, eight people injured in a Fiat Uno."

Malta had the second highest percentage of speed cameras in the European Union, but they did nothing to moderate maniacal road habits. Fatal accidents increased by 18 percent between 2001 and 2017, even as they decreased by 50 percent across the rest of the European Union. I could never figure out why everyone was in such a hurry. We lived on an island the size of a postage stamp. There wasn't anywhere to go.

"People drive in spurts," my friend said. "They'll go like a bat from hell one moment and then slam on the brakes to crawl past a speed camera. Everyone knows where they are, but you won't, so be careful. They can't judge speed when they see you coming either. You should expect other drivers to roll out blindly from side roads, lurching into your path and then crawling along. And be careful when overtaking. Count on them to drift out of their lane, especially on corners."

One-way streets couldn't be trusted. I routinely saw drivers go the wrong way through the roundabout in Zejtun because it was shorter. Horse-drawn carts blocked roads during rush hour, holding up enormous queues of traffic as the jockey stared straight ahead, oblivious to the honking and swearing that trailed for kilometers behind him. When the horse wasn't before the cart, it might be found crammed into the back seat of a compact car.

"When it comes to normal driving standards, expect nothing," my friend concluded. "You will get nothing less."

One piece of road wisdom seemed to hold true: showing courtesy was a sign of weakness. Right-of-way was decided by a hierarchy of bluff, bluster, tonnage, and expense. Vans and cars gave way to overloaded cement trucks, buses, and lorries—all of which probably had suspect brakes. Car drivers fought it out with a heavy foot on the accelerator and skillful use of the Maltese Look Away. And expensive dent-free BMWs and Mercedes gave way to everyone. The trick was to avoid eye contact with other drivers as you shoved your bumper into a roundabout before vehicles entering in the proper order could do the same. According to the Maltese Highway Code, the Look Away absolved everyone of personal responsibility. If no one sees you, how could you do anything wrong?

The obvious weakness in this strategy was that it relied on bluff and counterbluff. I quickly learned to raise the stakes by taking their favorite tactic one step further. In the classic Maltese Look Away, the other driver looks straight ahead, but I know he's watching me from

the corner of his eye, and he knows I see him. That's why, in my variation, I really did look away. As soon as we established contact and I
knew the game was on, I turned my head all the way to the right very
obviously and stomped on the gas. The other driver would slam on
his brakes, lay on the horn, and curse me out his window as I sailed
past. The outcome was as predictable as a salvo of petards. The key to
making my variation work is that you have to be willing to take a hit.
It is best applied when the other driver has a more expensive car.

I quickly mastered driving on the island, but I assumed a monotonous, lecturing tone behind the wheel. I hectored. I ranted. I couldn't
help but remark on everything I saw, and unlike the Maltese I took
it all very personally. But I did take secret delight in doing absolutely
anything I wanted without fear of punishment. I ran red lights in
front of cops. I drove as fast as the congested traffic would allow. I
swerved madly, mounted curbs, slalomed around lampposts, and cut
off other drivers at every opportunity, before they could do the same
to me. I told my wife I was just "going local," but in behaving this way
I became what I pretended to despise.

# DR. DALLI
# SPEAKS THE PAST

Like any small place, the island was full of local characters. One of my favorites was Dr. Dalli.

I dropped by his clinic at random one day to inquire about travel vaccinations. The door was unlocked, but the tiny reception room off the street was unstaffed. I followed the sound of voices down a narrow hallway to a room where a television bolted high on a wall was blaring what looked like a documentary about nomads. A man stepped out from behind a lopsided bookcase. He had a wrestler's build, with thick legs and a low center of gravity, and a shock of gray hair with an agenda all its own.

"Do you understand Mongolian?" I said, nodding at the scene of horseback eagle-hunting flickering across the screen.

"No, but it's very interesting. Did you know they live entirely on dried cheese and curd all summer? I've been calculating the nutrient balance of their diet…"

When I looked at my watch, an hour had passed. I'd forgotten why I went there in the first place, but I knew I'd be back.

Stopping by Dalli's clinic for a coffee and a chat was a crash course in the island's recent history. I could always rely on him to tell me those secrets I would never find in any book, because everyone chose to forget—or to conceal them from outsiders.

"I'm surprised you wanted to live in Zejtun," he said in the early days of our friendship.

"I was looking for someplace quiet," I said. "A village rather than the expat centers. Somewhere traditionally Maltese."

"You certainly chose the right place." He set down a dusty specimen jar, tightened the lid, and wiped his hands on his pants. "Don't you know its history?"

It was clear from his tone that I didn't.

"Zejtun was a Labour town. I never used to go to there during the Mintoff years. No one did. It wasn't safe for outsiders."

It was the first time I'd encountered the name of the Labour Party leader who shaped so much of modern Malta. The English-language history books mentioned him, of course, but they carefully avoided personal accounts of violence and corruption when talking about a man whose years in power were rife with it.

Dominic Mintoff drove deep wedges into Maltese society during his first stint as prime minister (1955–58) and leader of the socialist Malta Labour Party when he set out to break the power of the Catholic Church. The clergy resented Mintoff's attempt to separate church and state, institute civil marriage, and break their hold on censorship. Some feared the fiery leader and former Rhodes scholar might be a closet communist. As hostilities deepened and Mintoff dug in his heels, first in power and later from the opposition benches, Labour Party newspapers published frequent attacks against Archbishop Mikiel Gonzi and the church. Gonzi struck back by declaring voting Labour to be a mortal sin. His 1961 "interdiction" of the Labour Party executives saw them refused marriage, and Labour supporters refused marriage at the altar, though the latter could be married with less fanfare in the sacristy.

"People used to visit kiosks and buy copies of two different news-papers in those days. They'd carry the Nationalist Party paper openly and slip the Labour paper inside. It sounds funny, I know," Dalli said, shaking his head, "but being branded in this way caused real hurt."

Those who defied the interdiction and attended party rallies were declared *Suldati tal-Azzar* (Soldiers of Steel), a term that would be resurrected once more during our stay. The struggle tore families apart—Mintoff himself had a brother who was a priest—leaving an afterglow of bitter resentment still felt today.

Malta achieved independence from the United Kingdom in 1964 under the Nationalist Party government of Gorg Borg Olivier, and the church finally made an uneasy peace with the Labour Party in 1969. Mintoff was elected again with a one-seat minority in 1971 on a campaign ticket of clean, efficient government and an end to the patronage that marked the previous Nationalist administration. He promised *Malta L-Ewwel u Qabel Kollox* (Malta First and Foremost), and Labour really did transform the country during his first mandate. Mintoff introduced social benefits like the two-thirds pension, mini-mum wage, a children's allowance, and social housing. He created the national airline Air Malta, brought in civil marriage, put an end to the death penalty, and solidified the separation of church and state. For many poor Labour voters, Dom made them proud to be Maltese.

The anthropologist Jeremy Boissevain described him as "the tradi-tional Maltese father: aloof, mainly harsh, and looked after his own. The authoritarian figure was familiar to all Maltese. Most of them had grown up in and formed part of families dominated by such fathers."

Mintoff's authoritarian streak soon spiraled out of control. La-bour expropriated private property, nationalized the National Bank, forcing investors to hand over their shares without compensation, and closed the University of Malta's Faculty of Arts and Faculty of Science to silence dissent. But the first thing he set out to do after

returning to office was renegotiate Malta's financial agreements with
its former colonial ruler. It marked the beginning of the country's
break with Europe.

Mintoff wanted to squeeze more money out of the British for the
military bases they maintained on the island. He demanded a $33.8
million increase over the current rent of $13 million a year; a bold
move, given the island's vastly reduced strategic importance after
World War II. London was willing to raise the fees by $11.7 million
but no more. That was their final offer.

When "Deadline Dom" refused to budge, Whitehall sent a team
of "dismantlers" to start knocking down their facilities, and the 4,994
British residents stationed in Malta began leaving aboard Royal Air
Force VC-10s. Despite their obvious frustration with the Maltese
leader, the British left the door open for a final reconciliation. Defense Minister Lord Peter Carrington went as far as canceling a trip to
the Far East, ostensibly so he could supervise the withdrawal of British forces but in actuality to remain available should Mintoff choose
to return to the negotiating table.

"One of Mintoff's biggest brags, that he kicked out the British,
was just another lie spun by the Labour Party to hide his pathetic
bungling," Dalli said. "We only found out what really happened a few
years ago. He tried extortion, and they called his bluff and left."

In the end, the British simply walked away when their lease expired on March 31, 1979. Malta wasn't strategically important enough
for the price being asked or the headaches they had to put up with.

"Despite his tough talk," said Dalli, "fucking Mintoff begged them
to stay."

Declassified British secret archive phone transcripts show Deadline Dom pleading with British Prime Minister James Callaghan to
come to Malta for the base closure ceremony, to watch the flag go

down on behalf of Her Majesty—but only if he came as prime minister. Callaghan refused. The only foreign head of state who attended was Muammar Gaddafi.

As the deadline for full withdrawal of British troops approached, a Libyan air force cargo plane arrived at Luqa airport carrying forty-four men dressed in civilian clothes. When a government spokesman was questioned about this strange development, and about the wooden crates they were unloading, he insisted that the Libyans had come to run the airport when British air traffic controllers left. The crates contained technical gear, nothing more.

"Air traffic control in Tripoli and Benghazi was run by French and Egyptian technicians," Dalli said. "Everyone knew these guys were police and the crates were filled with weapons. Mintoff was terrified riots would break out the moment the English left."

Violence didn't break out, but mass unemployment did. With the closure of the British bases, Malta lost some twenty-two thousand full- or part-time jobs and an annual $54 million contribution to the economy. This sudden drop in revenue on an island without resources left the government in a serious bind. An increasingly desperate Mintoff picked up his begging bowl and set off on a world tour, playing Cold War rivals against each other in order to keep his country afloat.

"He acted like he was taking revenge," Dalli said. "If the West wouldn't give him money, he'd spite them by going to their enemies. The Russians, the North Koreans, Ceauşescu's Romania, the Chinese. It's such a Maltese thing to do."

Dom would find his greatest supporter close to home. Gaddafi had already loaned Malta some $3 million to replenish its dwindling social security fund. When the British left, this relationship with Libya grew. Malta played host to a Libyan college and to joint ventures with Libyan companies, and for a while the Arabic language was made a

compulsory subject in secondary schools. But this seemingly bottom-
less well of funds did not come without obligations.

The colonel gave Malta patrol boats and helicopters, but Gaddafi
also stationed a Libyan military unit on the island and started operating a Super Frelon helicopter from the Armed Forces of Malta (AFM)
base. He was training Irish Republican Army terrorists in Libya and
supplying them with arms trafficked through Malta, along with contraband cigarettes that provided the terrorist group with funds. And
when Libyan agents brought down Pan Am flight 103 over Lockerbie,
Scotland, in 1988, the bomb was loaded onto an Air Malta flight at
Luqa for transfer to the fated jet at Frankfurt.

"Malta became a province of Libya," Dalli said, scowling at a memory that was clearly still fresh. "Our government tailored policies to
fit Gaddafi's whims, and his enemies became our enemies. When
Libyan students were being hanged here, Mintoff's police passed the
murders off as suicide."

The United States and its allies feared that Malta would fall into
the Soviet sphere. A declassified CIA report from 1980 noted that
"the Prime Minister has become something of a folk hero for his role
in ridding the country of a foreign military presence. His forceful and
charismatic personality, his widely acknowledged skill as a political
organizer, and his tight grip on the dominant Labor Party put him at
a distinct advantage over his strongly pro-West but largely ineffective
Nationalist Party opposition." By 1986 the intelligence agency was
warning of "Malta's move to enhance ties to Libya and the Soviet bloc,
accompanied by an increasingly authoritarian style of government."

That special relationship with Libya never went away. I knew a
man who worked at a marina in the northern beach resort of Mellieħa
Bay. "Gaddafi's son came over here all the time before the war," he
told me. "My boss would get a call saying he was on his way, and we'd
be told to clear the entire place. We'd have thirty minutes to kick

out the customers. And then a speedboat would roar in, filled with
bodyguards and girls and Saif Gaddafi. He'd party all day, and then
he would leave."

"What did you think of it?" I asked. "Weren't you scared?"

"He always paid cash," my friend replied. "And he tipped us very
well."

The Labour years between 1976 and 1981 were marked by shortages of
essential items, electricity and water cuts, and rising political tensions.
Money flooded out of the country almost as quickly as the brain drain.
Those who couldn't leave legally moved to London, where they worked
in shops and hid behind counters to avoid the immigration police.

Dalli was a medical student in those years, first in France and then
in Greece. "Things got a lot harder after the British went," he told me.
"Mintoff closed the country and imposed currency controls on the
lira to keep money from bleeding away. He also restricted imports to
favor industries controlled by his friends. We could only buy one locally made brand of toothpaste, and foreign chocolate was forbidden.
We smuggled it in whenever possible. Passengers coming off every
ferry from Sicily were searched for contraband and shaken down for
bribes. Every time I went back to school in Athens, I had to sneak my
savings out in my socks."

He sat down on the edge of a stool and stared at the floor of his
office. "God, I loved it there. The Greeks are so passionate. They argue
and fight over everything, but they know how to laugh and drink too.
Everyone in Malta was looking over their shoulders in those days, so
afraid to speak out. Going back to Athens felt like freedom."

As corruption spiraled out of control, leading government politicians built up their own fiefdoms, with networks of dependent bu-
reaucrats, business interests, and hangers-on. The most powerful were
cabinet ministers who, in addition to government backing, controlled

their own constituency apparatus: an army of personal canvassers, bodyguards, enforcers, and fixers. Anyone who accepted a favor was compromised and could be leveraged for future favors or votes.

"If you needed a license or building permit, you had to get it through a bloody Labour Party connection," Dalli said. "Access to scholarships, medical benefits, and grants were controlled the same way. I didn't get one, of course." He shrugged and passed me another espresso. "My father was in the wrong political camp."

Supporters saw no distinction between the Labour Party and the government. They expected it to be biased in their favor, and they supported it fiercely. "There was never a sense of allegiance to state or nation in Malta," Dalli said, "or to anything larger than one's immediate blood relations. People supported their faction or party because it ran the government and had access to power that would be used to benefit their followers. Of course, this meant losing power was an existential threat."

It was no longer safe to be a critic of the regime.

"There were so many bombs in those days, we barely noticed," Dalli said. "Any time we heard an explosion, we'd say, 'Another bomb,' and go back to work."

I said the constant dread and repression made me think of North Korea. He knew I'd gone there a decade before to write my first newspaper column.

"Did you know the North Koreans trained our security services?" he said. "Really. It's true. The Labour government invited them in. They sent us mortars, small arms and antiaircraft guns, and four military officers to train Mintoff's elite Special Mobile Unit. Kim Jong-il studied English in Malta too, when he was young. He was a guest of Dom, though of course he lived here under another name."

The violence hit a new peak on October 15, 1979, a day that would come to be known as Black Monday, when thugs burned down the

*Times of Malta* building after attending a rally to mark Mintoff's thirtieth anniversary as Labour Party leader. A sergeant and five policemen were stationed outside Strickland House that day, but no one tried to stop the mob from battering their way in with a traffic bollard and smashing everything in sight. The fire raged for forty-two hours, consuming photos and documents and reducing large parts of the building to ash.

"I was in Valletta that day. Cops stood near Mintoff's office across the street and watched," Dalli said. "They didn't even call the fire department as the men doused the printing press and set it on fire."

The mob went from there to Birkirkara to ransack the home of Eddie Fenech Adami, the Nationalist Party leader of the opposition. His wife, Mary, returned from mass to find the front door open and ten men inside throwing books and furniture into the street.

"They were brandishing wooden clubs, solid legs sawn off a table," she said to a journalist years later. "I still have one in the garage somewhere. I call it the devil's club."

The men worked their way from room to room, smashing everything in their path until there wasn't a chandelier or light bulb left intact. Mary crept out and tried to close the front door, but this only sent the largest thug into a rage. "He slammed me against the wall, tried to rip my earrings off and slit my ear," she said. "He was punching me in the chest and face. Then he kicked and pushed me onto the street. I was beaten black and blue, but thank God he didn't break my bones or my teeth."

There was a police office on the same street, but again the police did nothing. Mary and her children escaped by crossing the rooftop to a neighbor's house. The perpetrators of these attacks were never brought to justice.

In the attack's aftermath, Mintoff accused the *Times of Malta* of "being in the pay of the foreigner" at Malta's expense. "That is why we could not keep our people from trying to break down the *Times*," he said to a crowd gathered in Floriana. "We did not send them, but we could not stop them." He also said "there [would] be trouble" if Labour lost the coming election, and if opposition leader Fenech Adami went on to sign the European Union accession treaty. "Yes, there will be trouble if this happens," he told the cheering crowd. "There will be trouble." It wasn't the first or last time critics of the Labour Party would be branded as "traitors to Malta."

The violence continued after Mintoff was replaced by Karmenu Mifsud Bonnici, but it was always Mintoff who pulled his puppet successor's strings.

Events reached a peak in 1986 when Nationalist Party supporters were authorized by the constitutional court to hold a mass meeting in Labour's Zejtun stronghold. Labourites worked all night to block the Tal-Barrani road with stones, rubble, and wrecked cars. When the Nationalists tried to enter the village for their legally sanctioned meeting the next day, a group of masked men stepped out from behind the barricades to fight them off.

The riot squad's Special Mobile Unit moved in, followed by mounted police and more than a hundred people, many of them armed. Shots were fired and tear gas deployed as the Nationalists were beaten back. One woman, Rose Gauchi, had her nose badly bitten. Salvu Debono was shot in the knee. Ten other men and five women sustained injuries serious enough to be reported. Six days later twenty-six-year-old Raymond Caruana was killed when someone sprayed the Nationalist Party club in Gudja with machine-gun fire.

No one was held accountable for what came to be known as the Tal-Barrani riot. The case finally made its way through the courts and a judgment was reached in 2002. The magistrate acknowledged that the events in Zejtun had taken place with the tacit approval of the police, who blocked the road, fired shots, and allowed armed and masked men to assist them. But it was all such a long time ago, and it's all in the past. Three men were conditionally discharged for their part in it, which the magistrate shrugged off as being connected to the political atmosphere of the time.

I spoke with one of the filmmakers behind the documentary *Dear Dom*, released five months before Mintoff's death in August 2012. "No one would talk to us," they said. "People would speak about him in secret, but they wouldn't be named or tell their story on camera, even with their faces obscured and their voices distorted." Grown men burst into tears describing the beatings they'd taken because they voted for the wrong party. Others told tales of businesses ruined, jobs lost, cars burned, and homes destroyed. But none were willing to speak out. "Dom may be dead, but many of the people who did these things to them are still there."

"That's Zejtun," Dalli said, poking me in the chest with a thick finger. "The town you live in. Labour never changes. The divide Mintoff made in our country is deep. Sometimes I look back at it all and wonder how we got through it."

"But why did you come back from Greece when you loved it so much?" I said.

He stopped for a moment and looked out the window. "I ask myself that every day."

We would eventually move to a different village halfway across the island. Less than a week after we left Zejtun, a man at the end of our block was murdered. Someone knocked on his door one February afternoon and shot him three times in the chest and neck. He died in the street, sprawled outside his front door—the very same door I could see from my roof. The man had been a bomb maker in the 1970s and 1980s, and he was still practicing his trade in that shabby garage. There were so many things going on behind those walls, things we as outsiders would never understand.

# CRACKS
# APPEAR

The newspaper was filled with a series of strange crimes that first summer, but people acted as though they were entirely normal.

Two old men in Gozo got into a heated argument over a parking space. The old man who had been robbed of a space climbed back into his heap of junk in a rage, drove around the block to build up speed, and ran the other old man down. He was given a suspended sentence for this vehicular killing because, in the words of the judges and lawyers, "Yes yes yes, but he was upset."

In another incident, a man pushed his wife down the elevator shaft of their building and ignored her cries as it took her several hours to die. In a country where walls act as amplifiers rather than soundproofing, how many neighbors heard her screams and did nothing?

On a different part of the island a criminal murdered another criminal father-son duo. When their bodies were found, the police discovered the murderer had buried them right on top of another man who had disappeared two or three years earlier, whom he had also been suspected of killing.

Violent assaults were a weekly occurrence in the "entertainment district" of Paceville, but they were rarely one-on-one. People only seemed to pick fights when the odds were three-on-one, or to hit or stab someone whose back was turned. It came as no surprise to learn that incidents of domestic violence—wife beating—were also common. These crimes provided a glimpse into a darker side of the island, but the fact that they were shrugged off as normal also revealed a strange sense of logic that seemed to exist outside the bounds of rationality.

My favorite crime—if one can be said to have a favorite crime—involved the theft of cigarettes. The island had a large free port near the town of Birżebbuġa, a massive dockyard of stacked containers and giant cranes, where cargo was unloaded from ocean-going ships and then reloaded onto smaller coastal vessels and sent to ports throughout the Mediterranean. Some cigarettes were stolen one night, but rather than take a few cartons, the thieves took an entire shipping container and brought it back empty the next day. Surely no one would notice?

Even the Maltese police, a group not known for their investigative prowess, had no difficulty solving this case. They simply looked at the logbooks and rounded up the only two people who had contact with the container and the guard who worked the front gate. Their conversation would have followed a typical pattern.

"Did you take a container of cigarettes from the port last night?"
"No."
"We have several eyewitnesses who said you did."
"No."
"We have you on video driving away with the container."
"No."
"Your own mother identified you. Did you do it?"
"Yes."

The only unusual element in this case was that the men eventually admitted it. They would normally deny right to the end, even in the face of irrefutable proof, and nothing could possibly convince them to say they were guilty. Professing complete ignorance of episodes that are common knowledge is still considered an excellent form of defense in Malta. And when all else failed, they would just get hold of a phrase to repeat louder and louder while shrugging their shoulders and flapping their arms.

Cars burned with alarming frequency too. I'd never seen so many vehicles spontaneously catch fire. There would be as many as four in one week. Part of this could be attributed to the fact that maintenance was regarded as a nuisance. Things continued to run until they didn't, and then it was time to deal with it. Cars and trucks gave up the ghost with great regularity in the middle of busy thoroughfares. There was no space to pull aside on roads hemmed in by stone walls, so the driver would get out, pop the hood, and crawl underneath, where he'd attempt to patch it together just enough to achieve forward momentum. Other drivers swerved around him, missing his legs by inches.

But it was only possible to attribute a certain percentage of these car fires to the total absence of preventive maintenance. They were often newer BMWs, not just the usual unmaintained wrecks. The newspaper reported that between 2011 and 2016, a total of 878 vehicles caught fire. When asked about this, the police helpfully offered that "the main causes of the noncrime vehicle fires are only established when all investigations and examinations are concluded."

At first I assumed everyone was torching their cars for the insurance money. Perhaps they were unable to make the payments on that nice shiny status symbol they'd coveted so strongly? But when one such car burned down during the night in the village of Xemxija, a neighbor said, "It was probably about the dog, ta. They had a very noisy dog. Their car was set on fire once before, and notes were left, but it still keeps barking." No one was ever caught for these crimes,

though there was never any doubt that the entire village knew who
did it.

My friend Charlie Vella shed some light on this. "People will com-
plain endlessly about some illegality, but they won't report it officially
because they don't want to testify in court so as not to make enemies."
He shrugged. "We like to dream of being a nation of brave hearts,
but in reality, cowardice masked as prudence is considered a positive
virtue. We'd like change to happen, but we're unwilling to expose ourselves to retaliation."

Like nearby Sicily and southern Italy, Malta is plagued by *omertà*—
that code of silence which says everyone should tend to their own
affairs and witnesses should never cooperate with the authorities. To
testify against a neighbor, even indirectly, exposes one to petty acts
of revenge from the culprit and from that person's family. Even criticizing government policy could result in loss of contracts for one's
business, refusal of a permit, or denial of promotion. The Maltese fear
of retribution was pervasive, and it resulted in a culture of collusion
through silence.

The island finally made international news in summer 2012 when a
photograph of a man being punched in the face went viral on the wire
services. It happened in the pretty little fishing village of Marsaxlokk,
a location that's heavily promoted in the tourist literature and a Maltese favorite for a Sunday fish dinner. It was just over the fields from
Zejtun, beyond the end of our street, and we went there often. But
like any village on the island, its normally peaceful surface concealed
turbulent undercurrents.

A local dispute had built to a boil in the August heat because a
group of squatters had completely taken over the beach at Il-Magħluq.
Rather than visit for the day, they'd brought in campers and erected a

sort of shanty town for the second summer in a row, and their numbers were growing.

Local residents complained they were being denied access to their
own beach. The squatters didn't have plumbing, so they ransacked the
public toilets like the Great Khan's armies on the march. They bought
their food and drinks from big discount chains like Lidl rather than
shop locally. And thanks to the Maltese penchant for litter, the area
was quickly becoming a rubbish heap. But the campers insisted they
weren't bothering anyone. All that rubbish simply washed up with
the current.

The people of Marsaxlokk finally had enough. Press photographers
happened to be there when a spontaneous protest against the squatters ignited a brief scuffle. Two shirtless thugs grabbed a protester by
the throat, backed him up against a van, and hit him in the face. One
image captures the sputtering rage of these men as the protester raises
his hands in defense and shouts for them to stop.

Law enforcement was lax at the best of times, but the image had
been picked up by the foreign press and couldn't be ignored. Four
men who were involved in the brawl were photographed sitting on the
courthouse steps the next morning. None wore the obligatory jacket
and tie required by Maltese courts. The elderly man who punched
the protester was wiry and darkly tanned in cutoff jean shorts; his
sleeveless T-shirt revealed a thick gold chain, and he wore enough
gold bracelets to give a Bedouin wife a run for her dowry. The man to
his right glared at the camera and stuck out his tongue as the others
laughed. The judge fined them €60 each. One man admitted he was
currently under a suspended sentence for a separate crime, but rather
than be remanded into custody, his suspended sentence was extended
by two years. This encouraged newspaper readers to speculate that if
€60 was the price of punching someone in the face, maybe it was time
to settle a few scores.

Like most things on the island the incident was quickly forgotten, and Malta's brief moment of international fame receded—at least until the next, much larger scandal broke. But nothing was done about the squatters. How could one village be singled out without opening a Pandora's box?

Nothing symbolized this more blatantly than the squatter community of Armier Bay. This gradually sloping stretch of beach sits at the far end of Malta, beyond the Marfa Ridge, where a chunk of land abuts the island like the top of an anvil. The views across the channel must be beautiful, with the bare rocky bulk of uninhabited Comino backed by the shoulder of green Gozo in the far distance. But the entire place has become a shantytown.

Squatters invaded Armier more than thirty years ago, and over the decades their numbers swelled, until this settlement of some eight hundred dwellings occupied an area equivalent to thirty-six football pitches. The boathouses they built, block by stone block, didn't house any boats at all. How could they? They were set back from the beach in a tight grid of streets. Most had electricity wired up illegally, until the government-controlled electrical authority decided to regularize these dwellings by installing meters in 2014. None of them had building permits, of course, or deeds of ownership for the land, so giving them government-supplied electricity was a tacit admission of their right to be there. The Enemalta power company argued it away by saying, "If we give them meters, they'll have to pay for the power they would otherwise steal." But this was just a backhanded way of buying votes from a block that had always supported Labour.

The Nationalist government issued some tough talk about the boathouses during our first year in Zejtun and even sent bulldozers to knock them down. But the boathouse owners barricaded the road and shouted obscenities; the police escorts stood there with their hands in their pockets and then walked away.

I asked Dalli why this was tolerated. "Flawed logic is the root cause of so many things that go wrong in this country," he said, tapping the side of his head with a finger. "The other causes are avariciousness, spite, ignorance, and stupidity. But of course, they're all interlinked. Anyone can get away with giving the finger to the law in Malta as long as there are enough people doing it."

Each summer, on a slow news week, when the illegalities of areas like Armier, Saint Thomas Bay, and Gnejna were raised, the boathouse owners came together to flex their muscles, screaming and shouting and acting as though someone was denying their God-given right to have a beach house. "You can't rip it down!" they'd shout. "I built it. Who's going to pay me for it?" Armier was a case study in how people abused the system, blatantly encroaching on the rights of others and then turning criticism on its head by portraying themselves as victims.

"The government talks about attracting high-end tourists," Dalli continued. "But what do they see when they arrive here?" He looked out the window and pointed with his chin. "Shanty towns. Campers. Broken infrastructure. And cranes and noise and dust."

Tomoko returned to the house, pale and shaking, early one afternoon.

"Did you get lost?" I asked, assuming she'd had a near miss in a roundabout on her way home. We'd been living in Malta for less than a year, and she still wasn't used to the maze of roads or the maniacal standards of local driving.

"Someone shot at me."

I laughed without meaning to. My first instinct was denial, not because I thought she was lying but because I didn't want to believe it could be true.

"Someone shot at me," she said again. And she went to the cabinet and poured herself a drink.

She had taken up photography when we moved to Malta from

Canada, illustrating my travel magazine features and doing local contracts for arts councils. She'd been photographing alone on the Delimara peninsula, a wild coastal area of isolated houses, farmland, and cliffs. We had gone walking there in spring 2011, down narrow dirt lanes set between stone walls running off from the smokestack of the power station and the remains of Fort Tas-Silġ. We explored broad stony flats carved with salt pans that looked like another planet, and we went swimming in its coves that summer. We didn't yet know Delimara was a hotbed of illegal bird poaching and trapping. To walk in the countryside during the hunting season—and to walk in the countryside in certain areas outside the legal hunting season—was to risk a confrontation with camouflage-clad armed men who automatically assumed any foreigner was spying on them for a European birdlife NGO. Incidents of tire slashing, verbal abuse, and fistfights were common. To carry a camera was even more damning evidence against you.

"I was taking pictures of our usual swimming spot," she said. "I heard two shots and felt something pass over my head. When I looked around I saw two hunters. They were standing in the distance holding guns, staring straight at me."

I tried to describe what gunshots sounded like at close range, convinced she'd mistaken it for fireworks or maybe the backfire of an aging car, but she was insistent.

"It had to be those hunters. The way they stared at me. . . . I got so scared I jumped in the car and took off." Her hands were still shaking half an hour later.

We were targeted more directly not long after this incident. There were two clay pots on either side of our front door with dark-green bay trees that lent a welcome slash of color to the streets clad in stone. We returned from the gym one day to find they'd been smashed, one after the other.

"How could someone drive into them and just leave without saying anything?" Tomoko asked. "Why wouldn't they tell a neighbor
or leave a note?"

"Because this was done on purpose. At least they didn't set the
front door on fire."

People had been parking their cars immediately in front of our
only entrance, completely blocking the door. Twice I had to climb
into the back of someone's pickup truck to get out the other side.
I'd left polite notes on windshields asking them to leave us enough
space to get in, but it never worked. The battle went on all summer.
I eventually spoke with the local council, and they sent someone to
paint a double yellow line in front of our gate, making it clear that
this narrow entrance was a no-parking zone, but the lines were gone
the next time we returned from a trip. A neighbor told me that right
after we left someone came along with a bucket of black paint and
simply painted them out.

I began to understand those villagers who paid to rent a garage.
They put signs on the door reading "Garage in use day and night." But
it didn't matter. Someone would double- or triple-park in front of it.
So they scrawled angry, threatening notes that read "Park here and
I'll smash your car." And when those, too, were ignored, they slashed
tires, smashed mirrors, and bent antennas in the night.

"No one here says anything to your face," I said. "Retaliation always
takes the form of some petty act of vandalism. The history books are
full of it. The smashed flower pots are a way of telling me to shut up
and stop complaining."

"Well, I guess we won't have to pick empty bottles out of them
anymore," Tomoko said.

I felt like the entire village was watching me through parted blinds
as I collected the broken pieces of clay in a cardboard box, put the
bay trees in a bucket, and carried them up to the roof. I didn't let

anything show on my face, but my outrage at being targeted in this way was slowly being replaced by a sense of rejection. We were quiet people who tried to be good neighbors, but we weren't wanted there; we were only tolerated.

Francis, an old man with a dazed and rather tortoise-like appearance, passed by as I was sweeping up the last of the dirt. "Oh no!" he said. "Your planter got broken."

"Someone drove into it."

"It must have been an accident," he said, with a pained smile. I spoke to Francis often when he passed our house, but this was the first time I'd seen his face assume what I recognized to be a mask.

"It was on purpose. No one could hit it accidentally without also driving into the wall. It must be because I complained about the parking."

His smile vanished. He stared straight ahead, said a few polite words, and continued on his way. The old lady across the road sat in her window watching me and didn't say anything at all.

# TRASH CAN
# AT WORLD'S END

In northern places trees lose their leaves in winter and the land takes on the barren appearance of death. This process was completely reversed in Malta, where winter rains brought intense greens, and where the summer sun burned the land brown and killed off anything less hardy than a prickly pear, a carob tree, or the seemingly indestructible olive. The only thing that felt inexhaustible was the dust. Northern dwellers endure the winter, suffering under a monotony of gray skies as they await the resurrection of spring. But in Malta it was the long weight of summer that demanded patience. In winter what we saw was not the Mediterranean of travel books but the sea of Ulysses pursued by a vengeful Poseidon.

Winters brought an ill wind that begat misfortune, incoherence, madness, and gusting passions. That's when the frigid northwest *majjistral* swept down from Europe, through the Alps and across the vast farms and hills of France, and over the open sea to Malta, where cold fingers sought out every crack in our wooden windows and every ill-fitted wooden door. Papers flew off tables, even with the windows closed. The temperature of the house dropped to that of a crypt. An army of propane heaters was powerless against it.

Most of the village houses had tall poles with blue lights on top, from which they would fly the flag of the band club during the festa or the flag of the country on national holidays. When the wind came up, the streets filled with the rattle and clang of pulleys and halyards. On the rare occasions when it stopped, I felt as though I had suddenly gone deaf.

Our palazzo was surrounded by alleys that never ran straight for long, which dissipated some of the *majjistral's* fury, but in the morning I'd find that the furniture on the roof had been shoved into a corner against the balustrades as though by an enormous hand. Once the cover of the jacuzzi was torn off completely. I found it on the kitchen roof, with plastic clips and screws still attached. Anything that had been left up there was jumbled and sometimes taken away, but never the olive trees or the ancient barrel cacti in their heavy pots. The olives bent their heads to the wind in grim endurance. Sometimes they sacrificed a few small fruits, but in the morning they were always there, leaves glistening silver in the dew.

Maltese houses were built for heat rather than cold, with high vaulted ceilings, tiled floors, and drafty wooden window frames. As the salty damp of sea air soaked into the walls, I spent those winter evenings huddled under a blanket with the cat, drinking Irish tea from heavy crockery, deeply absorbed in a book. The gas heater flickered and hissed, providing the barest illusion of warmth, as lashing rain fell from a bleak, gray sky and wind raged across hills barren of trees.

It was only when we walked in the garigue, that typical Mediterranean limestone scrubland with its rough stones and thorny plants, that I realized how intensely beautiful the island was, and how green it could be in winter.

I slipped an archaeological guide into a wide jacket pocket and we laced up our boots one sunny Christmas day to set out for Baħrija, a small rural village whose name means "moth" in Maltese. Everyone

else was eating with family or at a hotel buffet in the entertainment
zone, and for one afternoon the guns of the poachers had fallen silent.
Our objective was the isolated promontory of Ras ir-Raħeb, where
ruins lie partially buried at the far end of a flat point surrounded by
sea-plunging cliffs.

I spotted two upright megaliths from a distance, and we picked
our way toward them over clumps of grass littered with a surprising
amount of plastic and rusting shotgun shells. My boots crushed wild
thyme and scented our walk with the aroma of Italian cooking, and
the briny, stagnant water of a salt pan blew in on a coastal breeze.

The megaliths had been incorporated into a later site, but only the
grass-covered foundations remained. I paced the outline of a courtyard and walked down the center of what was once a wide corridor
with a room branching off, to where a rock-cut cistern shone a glint
of far-off water from the darkness below. Several objects had been
unearthed there: an ivory plaque with a crouching boar traced to
fifth-century Etruria; a pair of clay satyr masks; a male figure with a
lion skin tied around his waist; coins from the Sicilian Punic period;
and a late Roman coin depicting Constantine II. They gave a sense of
how many layers of the past intersect on the island, and how many
civilizations left traces on those rocky shores.

The oldest structures in Malta were the megalithic temples.
Erected during three distinct phases between 5000 BCE and 2500
BCE, they predated Stonehenge by a couple thousand years; even the
earliest pyramids of Egypt date to nearly a thousand years later. The
temple builders left little behind: a few fragments of pottery, a few
small carved statues, and the sculptural decoration on the temples
themselves. These remains reveal an extraordinary advance in their
art and architecture from 4100 BCE to about 2500 BCE, as though
they experienced a cultural flowering, and then suddenly, around
2500 BCE, the building stopped and every one of the temples was

abandoned for religious purposes. There are no signs of warfare, disease, or agricultural pressures. All that's known for sure is that they were gone.

The islands were deserted, and they remained empty until the Bronze Age peoples arrived. They left standing stones and the mysterious "cart ruts"—parallel channels worn or cut into the rock that ran for great distances in straight lines, ending at cliffs or the sea—but those people died out too, and all traces of them vanished.

The Phoenicians beached their beaked prows on Malta around the eighth century BCE, long after those Bronze Age people had piled stones into high defensive walls. The legendary seafarers built a temple at Tas-Silġ, near the present-day fishing village of Marsaxlokk, carved tombs into the rock around the town of Rabat, and used the island as a stopover on their sea-spanning trade routes. When the islands fell under the control of Carthage in the sixth century BCE, Malta continued to serve as a trading post between Sicily and North Africa. I imagined its markets filled with Carthaginian craftsmen, a place of woven cloth, dyed fabrics, gold jewelry, glassware, carved ivory, and gemstones. But Rome would soon clash with these North African upstarts.

Malta was raided by the Romans in 255 BCE, during the First Punic War, and by the Second Punic War it had fallen. Those linear, disciplined, legalistic people had ground their way around the Mediterranean with the relentlessness of a set of gears, conquering as far north as Hadrian's Wall. Not even Carthage's great hero, Hannibal Barca, could stand up against their plodding architectural strength forever.

Livy records that the islands were surrendered without resistance in 218 BCE to the consul Tiberius Sempronius Longus, who stopped by on his way to North Africa. Malta seems to have prospered during Roman times. The settlements that became present-day Mdina and Rabat grew to their maximum extent and were surrounded by defensive walls. The remains of a villa in the area, with floor mosaics indicating the wealth of the owner, date from the first century BCE to second century CE. Such dwellings have been found in other parts of the islands too, along with carved channels and foundations that indicate olive pressing. But despite being materially well off under the Romans, Malta was lumped together with Sicily and largely invisible in its shadow.

When the Western Empire finally crumbled and Gothic tribes fought the Byzantines for the remnants, Malta was likely occupied by eastern Roman forces. The general Belisarius landed there briefly in 533 on his way to North Africa. But until the Arab invasion, Malta remained a place of small huddled clusters of humanity that clung to the bays and spread over the remains of sunken mountains, buffeted by turbulent seas and events that sometimes washed up from the outside world.

Centuries of Arab slave raids embedded a fear of the countryside deep in the culture's collective memory. According to anthropologist Jeremy Boissevain, "until very recently the general public knew and cared very little about the countryside and were rather apprehensive about visiting it." To be in the towns was safer, jumbled up among others with the noise and the light and the anonymity of the herd. To be caught in the countryside after dark, even behind the walls of a sturdy farmhouse, was to invite fear. "They literally did not recognize its beauty and ecological importance," Boissevain continued. "Hence they were indifferent to its pollution and the destruction brought about by its privatization."

This indigenous fear of solitude was confirmed not long after we returned from a trip to Iceland, where I'd been working on a magazine feature. We'd spent a couple weeks exploring the uninhabited central highlands in a four-wheel drive, camping and walking and seeking connection with the land, and when we returned a friend suggested we meet an expat teacher who had lived there for a year with her Maltese husband.

"My in-laws came to visit us once," she told me over coffee at the airport café. "We took them for a drive down the Ring Road to the west. You know what it's like. The countryside is like a beautiful other world. But my Maltese father-in-law started getting nervous as soon as we left the suburbs of Reykjavík. He kept looking out the windows and behind us. And then he turned to me and said, 'I don't like this... I don't like it... Where are all the people?' He panicked and we had to take him back to the city. He was terrified to be alone out there, but we were just outside town."

Of all the theories proposed for the clifftop ruins of Ras ir-Raħeb, the one I'd like to believe is that it was a sanctuary of Hercules. Like the Phoenicians who came before them, Carthage was associated with the worship of Baal, who fertilized the earth with his seed, dying each year with the annual harvest to be reborn again in the spring. His sacred precincts were high places—mountaintops, places of child sacrifice, the spot where the biblical Abraham offered his son Isaac to his god. Baal was paired with Tanit, sister-lover of many names—Ishtar, Astarte, Aphrodite—a dweller of groves and freshwater springs, which might explain the existence of the cistern behind me. From the Phoenician Melquart to Carthaginian Baal to the Roman Hercules. Like the island itself, this tiny site of standing stones was layered with civilizations, and with temples erected to metamorphosing gods.

Such a temple would have been visible far out to sea; an important landmark for ancient mariners crossing between North Africa and Sicily. I tried to imagine sighting it from a creaking square-rigged ship as we sat in the shade of the megaliths and opened a packet of peanuts and two cans of beer. Late-December waves crashed against the base of the cliff, painting resonant portraits in moving white foam. Gozo huddled green in the far distance, and the vast, empty sea stretched

all the way to Libya. But it was difficult to block out the present. The
access path we'd walked in on bisected the land of a local farmer, and
aggressive hunters had taken over the rest. Stone bunkers covered
in scavenged sheet metal and ragged tarps dominated the landward
view, and the entire scene bristled with aggressive Keep Out signs and
red-painted RTO (*Riservato*) warnings.

I spotted a path on the edge of the promontory and followed it
down the hillside, where broad shelving flats of smooth stone lined
the clifftop leading away from Ras ir-Raheb. A series of shallow foot-
holds had been carved into the rock, next to a badly weathered rope,
which led to another shelf of stone farther down. We reached a dead
end where a finger of water had carved an inlet, surrounded by cliffs
on three sides, but it was narrow enough to leap across, onto a ledge
beneath a low overhang of stone.

Those minor obstacles protected another world: an isolated ex-
panse of wind and solitude, where the cliff dropped to depths inhab-
ited by pelagic fish like tuna and shark. A series of shallow salt pans
had been carved into the rock next to perfectly round boreholes and
a narrow-stepped passageway that had been cut to the sea. No one
knew how old the pans of Blata Tal-Melh were, but crystals of salt still
collected in the sun when sea-heaved spumes sprayed from those deep
man-made holes. In winter, the waves coursed even higher. Behind us,
a plaque had been attached to the rock face in memory of a fisherman
who had been swept off that shelf by heavy seas in the 1960s.

It was only after we'd spent an hour at the site that I realized we
hadn't seen any wildlife at all, apart from one black beetle. When the
wind died down, it was replaced by total silence. In Malta the towns
sing with noise, and the countryside is silent except for the wind.


I'd noticed the old lady across the road watching me when I slipped
outside at 2 a.m. to put out the trash before we went to bed. I would

see movement behind the slats of lit shutters, and then her window would open slowly. It happened more often when the summer heat was at its worst. I was careful to pretend I didn't know she was there. Sometimes a full moon shone down on our alley, and I stopped for a moment to look at it because I liked the way it made me feel, so late at night and so alone. She watched me at those times too, and I thought I sensed her judgments change.

And then one winter day we parked our car next to her window. The sidewalk always reeked of ammonia because she fed a community of cats. One of the regulars, a three-legged stray, hobbled around the corner as Tomoko was closing her door. She turned to the old lady without thinking and said, "Poor kitty! What happened to her leg?"

"She had an accident," the lady replied, in perfect English. "A car."

It wasn't as though a mannequin had suddenly made cryptic utterances. She spoke as though she'd never not talked to us.

"Did the car cut her leg off?" Tomoko asked, concealing her surprise much better than I hid mine.

"No, she was hurt. I took her to a doctor." The cat must have sensed we were talking about it, because it hopped up to the window, slithered once around the old lady's arm, and vanished inside.

"She's very agile!" Tomoko said, and the lady's face lit up in the nicest smile.

From that day on, she smiled and waved every time we left the house. I had taken her abrupt dismissals as dislike, or maybe even a hatred of foreigners, but it may have been the shyness of a villager unused to dealing with outsiders. My own introversion should have clued me in to that.

I asked Marian's father, Peter, about her the next time he stopped by. "Her name is Sinjura Spiteri," he said. "She used to be a schoolmistress. She's always lived in that house. She used to live with her sister, but the sister died years ago."

We were abroad for most of December, and there was something strange about our neighbor's place when we returned. Someone was refilling the tin plate below the window for her cats, but the house had changed. It felt as though it had closed in on itself.

She'd been taken to hospital while we were away and died a couple weeks later. My friend the barber told me her house was broken into the very same day. "It was probably her relatives," he said. "It happens often here. They don't want to wait for the will to go through the courts. They're afraid they'll be cut out or that someone else will get the things they want." He shrugged. "She had a lot of antiques. Everyone knew."

That first island winter we were invited to share Christmas Eve dinner with Marian's family. She lived in a flat along Sliema's promenade, in one of the few older buildings still standing in an area that used to be a seaside retreat but had since fallen under the jackhammer of rapacious builders with their generic concrete cubes.

We gathered in her dimly lit living room, where the flicker of propane heaters competed with Advent candles to give the illusion of warmth. Tomoko and I sat off to the side as the family exchanged Christmas presents. Their gifts were simple and artistic, just a book or something made by hand. It was so different from the Christmases I remember as a child. Our tree was heaped with presents, as though my mother hoped to buy happiness despite the strained relations in our home. I usually slipped off to my bedroom at the earliest opportunity to listen to a new record or read a new book, but this family leafed through their books together, and Peter spoke to his grandchildren and asked their opinions about art.

When Marian's younger brother and his fiancée arrived, we moved to the dining table. As the food was passed around, Veronica, the fiancée, picked up the bread basket and said, "Maltese bread is the best in the world."

This would normally be an uncontroversial topic in Malta, and everyone would agree, but Marian's family was widely traveled and her children had lived abroad. "What are you talking about!" they said, all speaking at once. "Maltese bread is thoroughly mediocre."

"You've obviously never been to France or Germany."

Marian cackled with a volume that rattled spoons and brought plaster falling from the ceiling; somewhere in Gozo an old lady dropped her bread roll and looked around in alarm. Veronica staggered back under this bombardment of sarcasm as her bid for popularity turned into its opposite.

As his fiancée was being teased by everyone for her opinions about bread and her poor grasp of the Maltese language, her betrothed tugged me by the sleeve, leaned his head close to mine, and whispered, "I collect Nazi memorabilia. Isn't that terribly naughty?"

The New Year arrived unnoticed, and several weeks passed. And then one January morning the doorbell rang and I was served with a summons. I was ordered to appear in front of the local tribunal for nonpayment of a traffic fine.

"But I haven't received any tickets," I said.

The process server shrugged and walked away.

"What do you think it could be?" Tomoko asked.

"I wonder if it has something to do with that crumpled paper I found on the car?"

We'd gone abroad to do a feature for a travel magazine, and I had left the car in its usual place in front of the house. There was a ragged scrap of paper on it when we returned three weeks later, faded by the sun and crusted with dust. I fished it out of a drawer and compared it with the summons.

"That's it, all right," I said. "It's a ticket. It accuses me of driving the wrong way up a one-way street. I assume they mean this street."

"But that's impossible. We were in Africa."

I set to work preparing my case. I would represent myself at the local tribunal, where I'd set the scene with dramatic flair. Then, just as tensions reached their highest point, I'd whip out copies of our air tickets and boarding passes, proving that we could not possibly have been seen driving the wrong way down a one-way street. We were thousands of kilometers away. Someone had either made a stupid mess of that ticket, or—more likely—were just trying to get a payment out of me, since the car was sitting in front of my house the entire time. Counselor, magistrate, members of the television audience, I rest my case.

The morning of my court date finally arrived. We drove across town to the tribunal, and I presented my summons. We were told to wait in an anteroom until we were called.

"How long does it usually take?" I asked.

The lady shrugged and turned back to her computer.

The small, windowless waiting room held all the nervous anticipation of a dentist's office without the expired magazines. Men tugged at confining collars. A lady mopped her brow with a scented handkerchief. One guy dabbed at a shaving cut on his chin. The only sound of shuffling paper came from the pages of the book I'd brought along. We were the only foreigners in the room, and I wondered if we could be the only foreigners ever to appear before this tribunal. It certainly seemed that way from the covert glances the others were aiming at me.

"What's that noise?" Tomoko whispered.

"Shouting," I said. It was coming from inside the tribunal chamber. The defendant seemed to be shouting at the judge, and the judge and a policeman were shouting back.

When my turn finally came, we walked inside and stood behind a worn brown table with folding metal legs.

"Ryan Murdock of Triq Santa Marija, Zejtun?"

"I am."

"It says here that you're accused of overspeeding," the judge said, "and you failed to pay the fine."

"But that's not right, " I said, momentarily thrown into confusion. "The ticket I received—I have it here—it says I was driving the wrong way—" I fumbled to pull it out of a folder bulging with boarding passes, reservations, and a glossy magazine.

"Wait a moment," she said, looking more closely at her papers. "Wait a moment.... No. No, it's all right, you can go."

"Excuse me?"

"The date is wrong. The year is 2011, but this ticket says 2012. It's dated one year in the future." She shrugged. "You're free to go."

"But that's not the issue at all," I tried to say. "The ticket wasn't right in the first place. I wasn't even in Malta.... We were in Africa—" But no one was listening. "Don't you see? I've been framed," I wanted to say, "I'm an innocent man!"

I tried to exhibit my carefully assembled proof, but it was impossible for anyone to hear me because the entire courtroom had broken into laughter. The judge was laughing. The man on the bench beside her was laughing and shaking his head. Even the policemen and the stenographers were laughing. We stood there frozen, stunned into immobility as what began as a light chuckle grew into generalized cackling.

"You don't understand," the man on the bench said, waving my ticket in the air and wiping a tear from his eye. "You're free to go!"

Through a voice choked with laughter, the judge said, "It's your lucky day!"

"My god," I said, turning to Tomoko. "This is exactly what Kafka was writing about."

I heard the judge banging the gavel spasmodically as we backed out the door.

We walked through the garden to our car, severely dumbfounded.

"Malta is a country in which normal and abnormal are completely inverted."

"I think we'd better have a drink," Tomoko replied.

# THE ISLAND IS DEAD,
# SURVIVING ON MEMORIES

The past I was discovering diverged more and more from the present state of the island, but it also diverged from the "ideal" past that was told to casual visitors. Like those family stories meant to keep up appearances, Malta had a different history that wasn't advertised to outsiders. It was like your friend's Uncle Larry, "living temporarily" in a basement room that reeked of armpits and weed, the uncle everyone knew wasn't really looking for a job. But Malta's secret history wasn't just down on its luck. Its foundational myth of resistance to Arab conquest, and an unbroken history of Christianity dating back to the apostle Paul, seemed to be based on a lie.

"I've uncovered a vast conspiracy," I said, walking into the kitchen one morning for a cup of coffee.

"What, not another one?" Tomoko said.

"Make fun of me all you want, but look at this." I handed her a book about Maltese history. It was part of a four-volume set that included a guide to the remains from each period, and it was widely available in every tourist shop on the island.

"What am I supposed to see?"

I stacked the other books on the table. "The temple period and prehistory—one volume. The Roman, Phoenician, and Punic periods—one volume. The medieval period—one volume. And the time of the Knights of Malta—one volume. You've studied the history. Now tell me, how long was the period of the knights?"

"Is this a quiz?"

"It was 268 years. They took possession of the islands in 1530 and handed them over to the French in 1798. Okay, how long was the period of Arab rule?"

"I don't know. That was pretty minor. They were here for a while, but so was everyone else."

"Wrong. The Muslim conquest of Malta took place in 870. The period didn't end until the second Norman invasion of 1127, but Muslim communities still formed the bulk of the population for quite a long time after that. Got a calculator?"

"I don't need one. That's 257 years. Almost as long as the time of the Knights."

"Only eleven years' difference," I said, and pointed at the books on the table. "That four-volume history of Malta is 938 pages long, but it only contains fourteen pages about the Muslim period. The entire book on the medieval centuries talks about Byzantines and Angevins, Normans and Catalan-Aragonese. Just footnotes by comparison."

"But Catholic footnotes."

"Now do you believe me about the conspiracy?"

In his 1885 novel *Mathias Sandorf*, Jules Verne wrote:

The Maltese are Africans.... It is said that all the men are alike, copper in color, with slightly wooly hair, with piercing eyes and robust and of medium height. It seems as if all the women were of the same family, with large eyes and long lashes, dark hair, charming hands.... The Maltese have the mercantile instinct.... Hard-working, thrifty, economic, industrious, sober, but violent, vindictive and jealous.... They speak a dialect of which the base is Arabic...a language animated and picturesque, lending itself easily to metaphor and poetry.

But the Maltese looked down on their neighbors in the Maghreb. I was told they saw themselves as akin to Sicilians, justifying their northern orientation by a long, unbroken allegiance to Catholicism, but the feeling was not mutual. I met a Sicilian wine grower once at a festival in Berlin. "Malta is a very strange place," he told me. "I've been there several times. They're very good at attracting tourists. But the food is terrible. Terrible."

"I really thought it would be better," I said. "Closer to Italian food."

"Of course not! Maltese are Arabs," he said, and walked away.

According to historian Mark Camilleri, the prevailing view, espoused by the church and reinforced by the university, was that the modern Maltese population had largely originated in Sicily and had clung to their faith despite waves of Islamic conquest. This view was accepted for generations by an illiterate people who relied on church schools for their education, but Camilleri claims it was not reflected in the documents. It would take a stubborn scholar known for contrary thinking to bring those documents to light.

Historian Godfrey Wettinger stirred up a career's worth of popular ire when he researched the Muslim period, picking his way through primary sources buried deep in the archives and studying Arabic documents beyond Malta to understand what was happening in the region at that time. His work would challenge the story of Malta's unbroken history of Christianity.

Wettinger claimed that the Maltese islands were entirely depopulated after the Muslim-Tunisian invasions of 870. Some inhabitants were undoubtedly killed, and some taken away to be sold as slaves, but the islands were left completely deserted, a place of empty buildings and rotting bones. This is well attested by the accounts of sailors who stopped there to take on water or wood. They reported the remains of abandoned towns where wild sheep and donkeys roamed free. According to Wettinger, the Muslim people of the Maghreb only resettled the islands in the late 900s, repopulating them from zero, and they would remain under Muslim control for another 257 years.

But Malta had too many sheltered harbors too close to Sicily to leave it in Saracen hands. The Normans finally invaded in 1127, and the islands became part of the Kingdom of Sicily for the next 440 years. Christians returned, expanding the population through immigration from Sicily and through the stationing of Norman garrisons, but they were still outnumbered by Muslim families for a very long time, as Wettinger demonstrated through census reports and through his studies of the language.

By 1240, some 150 years after the first Norman raids of 1091 had resulted in an annual tribute paid to Count Roger of Normandy, the official records of Messina give the number of "Saracen" families in Malta as 836, Christian as 250, and Jewish families as 39. Malta didn't become Christian again until 1248, when the Norman emperor Frederick II—the current and rather distant ruler of the islands—ordered all Muslims living within his dominions to convert or leave.

The cultural continuities were strong enough that the island's Arabic-derived language was not significantly altered or eradicated by the purge. Traces of the original Arabic remain in the names of Maltese towns, as clearly Semitic as the place-names of Sicily are Sicilian. We see it too in common Maltese surnames that came down from Arabic, like Caruana, Farrugia, Mintoff, Muscat, Saliba, Sultana, and Zahra. Even the hood that Maltese women used to wear—a garment halfway between a Muslim burqa and a Catholic nun's wimple—suggests an evolutionary transition.

But Wettinger's version of the story was a message many people didn't want to hear. Paint was thrown on the front door of his house, and he received so many threats that he finally stopped publishing on the topic. The backlash he endured for writing about the Muslim period wasn't worth it.

Malta was richer for its Arab past. Even the best of their delicacies—figs, almonds, sweet pastries, and spices—had their origins in this period. I couldn't understand why people seemed so ashamed of that part of their heritage. Why wouldn't they want to learn more about it, rather than cover it up and get angry at anyone who mentioned it? It isn't as though they had anything to lose. The origin story for their unbroken history of Christianity didn't seem to be true either.

Saint Paul was said to have brought Christianity to the islands when he was shipwrecked there in 60 CE on his way to Rome from the Holy Land, and the Maltese people had been Christian ever since. But they weren't your run-of-the-mill church-on-Sunday Christians. They were on the front lines, forming a bulwark between the true faith of Europe and the Muslim world, saving Christianity as they had always done and will always do. Every Maltese child was told this story from the moment they were old enough to be told anything, and everyone repeated it.

The entire basis of this belief was a single line from the Bible: "And when they were escaped, then they knew that the island was called Melita" (Acts 28:1). The book of Acts goes on to say that Paul had washed up on an island where the people were barbarous but kind. A fire was lit for him, and when Paul reached out for a bundle of sticks he was bitten by a snake. "No doubt this man is a murderer," the islanders said. "Though he hath escaped the sea, yet vengeance suffereth not to live." But Paul shook the snake off into the fire, and nothing happened. When he didn't keel over dead or balloon up with poison, the island's inhabitants changed their opinion. He must be a god.

The chief man of the island, Publius, heard about this feat and invited the castaways to lodge with him. Paul healed Publius's feverish father and went on to heal other islanders as well. Then they left. The last verse reads: "Who also honored us with many honors; and when we departed, they laded us with such things as were necessary. And after three months we departed in a ship of Alexandria, which had wintered in the isle, whose sign was Castor and Pollux."

That's it. Eleven vague and inconclusive biblical verses. Malta wasn't even the only Melita in the Mediterranean at that time; several islands shared the name. But the Christian practice of repurposing earlier pagan stories in order to win converts would be put to good use.

Historian Mark Camilleri writes that there was a local sea-related cult in the area of what is now Saint Paul's Bay. It had existed for centuries before the Knights of Malta's arrival, a superstition associated with fishermen and the old gods. According to Camilleri, a Maltese Jesuit priest called Girolamo Manduca caught wind of it in the sixteenth century. He was familiar with the brief mention of Saint Paul's shipwreck in the Bible and the coincidence of all those islands called Melita, and he set out to stoke the fires of the faithful by grafting the Christian story onto this much older one. The priest would dedicate his life to propagating the idea that this fisherman's cult was in fact the story of Saint Paul washing up on Malta.

Camilleri describes how the Jesuits took up Manduca's story with enthusiasm. It was repeated by an Italian, Giovanni Francesco Abela, in 1647 and published in his *Descrittione di Malta*. The Catholic Church in Malta used this Italian book as documentary proof of the legend—even though the author heard it from them—and they cranked up the propaganda presses and repeated it until it became common knowledge. When Maltese people did try to promote their own indigenous beliefs—superstitions like the fear of the evil eye or folk remedies—the church hauled them before the Inquisitor to be tortured back into line.

The Saint Paul legend was deeply entrenched in the Maltese psyche and was used by both the church and the state to consolidate their rule, but in 1987 German theologian Heinz Warnecke dealt it a staggering blow. He claimed, in his doctoral thesis "The Real Journey to Rome of the Apostle Paul," that the famous shipwreck mentioned in the Bible had happened on the Greek island of Cephalonia, not Malta.

This man was simply an obscure academic studying an obscure event in an old religious text, but he had inadvertently kicked a hornets' nest. Anthropologist Jon P. Mitchell recounted what happened when the Maltese eventually caught wind of this dissertation. Warnecke's findings were published in the *Sunday Times of Malta* in February 1989, and he was invited to Malta that May to explain himself in a public forum. It must have felt a lot like being called to the principal's office for a scolding.

He was pitted against Dun Ciarlo, a prominent priest from Saint Paul's church. The evening began on a friendly note, but clerical tempers soon flared. The priests argued that because Warnecke was an outsider, he was unqualified to comment. Several spectators also pointed out that Warnecke had never been to Malta before he wrote his thesis. The priests conceded the absence of solid documentary or archaeological evidence for Christianity in Malta before the fourth century, but Dun Ciarlo insisted that "you just have to be Maltese to know that Saint Paul was shipwrecked here."

Much to the surprise of the entire assembly, these impassioned arguments did nothing to change the German scholar's mind. That's when opinion shifted. This was an offense against the entire nation. A malicious attack on Maltese identity. Yet another example of a large country bullying a small one. Believers were being told something they didn't want to hear, and their response was not to refute the proof but to cry, "You're attacking me!"

This same line of argument would soon be leveled at outsiders, from international press freedom groups to the Council of Europe, who tried to hold Malta accountable to the rule of law.

THREE

# DAPHNE

# MADONNA!
# WHAT HAPPENED?

On March 11, 2013, the Labour Party returned to power after twenty-five years in the political wilderness. They won by thirty-six thousand votes, an unheard-of majority. Memories of the repressive Mintoff period had faded, the status quo had gradually gone stale, and even people who should have known better were clamoring for change. The challenger, Joseph Muscat, ran on the same early Mintoffian platform of good governance, transparency, and meritocracy, but with a slick new social media campaign that rebranded Labour as a "movement" while barely mentioning Labour at all. It happened so quickly that no one questioned where this campaign came from or how they had so much money to fund it.

The Maltese were told to have the "courage to vote Labour" for the first time, because "Malta belongs to all of us" (*Malta taghna lkoll*). And the new thirty-nine-year-old prime minister seemed to offer a breath of fresh air after so many years of complacent Nationalist Party governance. Of course, when cornered, he glared like an aspiring Mussolini with tilted jaw and blazing eyes, but this *duce*'s chin was lost in the roundness of his face. It's difficult to be intimidating when one is so short. He reminded me of a sulking child, and I regarded his self-important tantrums as ridiculous. But Muscat was a disciple of Mintoff, and we would soon learn he was cut from similar cloth.

The changing of the guard asserted itself in our personal lives almost immediately. One morning not long after the election, Tomoko returned from her errands, puzzled. "The lady at the pharmacy is gone."

"What do you mean, gone?" I said.

"You know the pharmacy down past the police station, where I've been shopping for the past two years? The staff has completely changed. When I asked a clerk where the other lady was, she just said, 'Gone.' I asked her if the business was sold, but she said, 'No, no, no. There was an election.'"

I spoke with a friend from Heritage Malta a couple of weeks later. "Do you know anyone with access to Fort Ricasoli?" I asked. "I know it's controlled by the Mediterranean Film company, but I'd love to get a look inside."

"I used to know someone, but he's not there anymore," he said, and shrugged. "The election."

Dr. Dalli confirmed it. "Everything changes after an election. Voting here is transactional. Everyone's looking for something for themselves. A night watchman's job where they can punch the clock and go to sleep, or a building permit, or maybe a contract. When an election happens and power changes hands, the government removes the supporters of the other party and fills every position with supporters of their own."

"But is that even legal?"

He just shrugged. "This is Malta. Both sides do it."

And so the country ground to a halt for months as an entire bureaucracy of unqualified people, many with no background or education in their new field, tried to figure out what they were supposed to do. The day-to-day changes we saw after the election made me realize there wasn't a single institution in the country that didn't come

under the thumb of the party that had just taken over. Economist
Paul Caruana Galizia told me it had always been this way. "Public
sector corruption has long been a problem in Malta," he said. "When
the [British] colonial government took over the operation of the
country's grain trade, run by a central body called the *Universita* (the
knights had monopoly power over it), the governor described it as a
'dunghill of corruption' and vowed to liberalize the trade but never
really managed. The colonial service became a vehicle for nepotism
and clientelism, where public sector employment was used to buy loyalty. The most problematic were the naval dockyards—the country's
single biggest employer for a long time, although they were extremely
unproductive. There were also seriously high levels of tax evasion and
corruption in public tendering and nationalization, especially in the
1970s and 1980s."

The Maltese world was divided into hostile camps in a winner-
take-all political game dominated by clientelism, nepotism, cronyism,
and open trading in influence for votes. Politics was an end in itself.
You didn't run for office because you wanted to make your country
better or to serve. You ran because of what you could get, and your
supporters voted because of what you could give them personally if
you won. This went a long way toward explaining Malta's remarkably
high voter turnout.

Friends, relatives, or patrons in government obtained building permits, regularized illegal buildings, secured government jobs and contracts, or influenced the courts in return for loyalty, political support,
cash, or favors. Even the police were not immune to this cycle. As Carmel Cassar writes in *A Concise History of Malta*, "ministers of the various ruling political parties strove to recruit persons on whose personal
loyalty they could depend. The net result was that those appointed did
not consider themselves as civil servants but as party henchmen."

When the country was on the verge of joining the European

Union, arguments were made that such practices should be stamped out if Malta was to develop into a fully modern democracy, but there was great anxiety about what would happen to the people if clientelism were abolished. How could they possibly survive? When objections were raised to these practices, the response was a strange sense of Maltese exceptionalism: We're a small country; the same standards shouldn't apply to us. And besides, it's unfair because we're victims of colonialism. But the idea that it's never your fault, you're always a victim, and someone else—the British, the other political party—is to blame robs you of the power to shape your own future.

Behavior that would cause massive scandals in the rest of Europe soon became so normal on the island that the media didn't report it. Opposition to corruption was seen by red Labour supporters as nothing more than petty jealousy on the side of the blue Nationalists. They said that when the Nationalists eventually got back into power, it would be their turn to exploit the same network. No one would be prosecuted because there seemed to be an unwritten rule in Maltese politics that you get to keep what you made while in office. In the fifty-two years since independence, not a single Maltese politician had ever been convicted of corruption.

The election of Joseph Muscat seemed to portend something ominous. Economically, the country was on the rise, but I felt a growing sense that bounds were slipping. I'd laughed at the fuss over the divorce referendum and billboards that read "What would Jesus think?", and I clipped articles about the doomed attempt to overhaul the bus system. Things bumbled along and often went wrong, but it all sort of worked itself out. The sense that "It'll all be awl-right, just take a rest or go to the beach" was part of the island's charm. But when Labour returned to power in 2013, things took a darker turn.

The usual carcades had swept through our village when the election results were announced, but their jubilation was tinged with hostility. Dr. Dalli described it as a sense of payback. "'It's our turn now,' that's what they're feeling. 'You held power for twenty years, but we're in charge now and we intend to take what's ours.' Mark my words, it won't end well. We've been down this road before."

Muscat was thirty-nine, young and charismatic, a breath of fresh air after the stiff, toupee-encrusted Alfred Sant and the tired nine-year reign of Lawrence Gonzi. Voting had traditionally gone along hereditary lines—one's family was staunchly Nationalist or Labour, and like one's football team or band club, you supported the party your father and grandfather supported before you, unless you were young and rebellious, convinced by Muscat's slick vision of change.

Labour ran a sophisticated campaign the likes of which had never been seen on the island. Muscat promised meritocracy, transparency, an end to cronyism, but also the right to be whoever you wanted to be, even if it meant being gay or divorced. It all sounded so good on paper. Only the older generation who had lived through the Mintoff years were warning that Labour would never change.

The first indication of murkiness came early on, when Muscat announced he would lease his own vehicle to himself. He was entitled to a prime ministerial car and driver, but he would save the state unnecessary expense by continuing to use his own aging Alfa. Sure, he'd still have a driver, and the little Maltese flag he stuck on the corner of the hood was a vain affectation, as were the motorcycle outriders whose wailing sirens and flashing blue lights cut a privileged swath through the island's increasingly congested traffic. But Muscat was arrogant enough to try to get away with what was in effect turning down a government car so he could be paid an additional €7,000 per year—plus a generous petrol allowance—to use his old beater as his official limo. His supporters defended him with the predictable fervor of "my team versus your team," though they were getting screwed no differently than taxpayers on the other side of the divide. When he brazened it out, Muscat knew he could get away with anything.

I didn't follow the press in those early years, except to laugh at some of the stranger stories, until an elderly Maltese friend shamed me one afternoon over coffee when his conversation revealed my ignorance of current events.

"What, you don't read the *Times*?" he said, his voice tinged with disappointment. I had to admit I did not.

Somewhere around the end of 2013 I started paying attention to what was happening in the country we now called home; not just the small details of village life but the current state of the nation. The newspapers were sold by the time I left my desk each day, so I looked online. And at some point, in a moment of despair, I stumbled across the *Running Commentary* blog by Daphne Caruana Galizia. To cite her name was to take sides in the ongoing village football match that is Maltese politics. Even Dalli looked over his shoulder and whispered when he asked, "Do you read Daphne?" She was reviled by half the country and secretly loved by the other half, but everyone followed her—especially her enemies.

I first came into direct contact with Malta's fiercest journalist much later, in January 2017, when she reposted an article I'd written about the island for a Canadian travel magazine. I opened *Running Commentary* one morning for what had long become my daily read and saw my name at the top of the page. The headline was inflammatory—"Malta, a developing country riddled with corruption and dirt"—and for a second I felt what so many Maltese politicians must have felt: exposed, wary, caught out.

I received an email from my publisher moments later. "I don't know what's happening," he said, "but one of your old articles just went crazy. We've never seen such a spike in traffic."

"Get ready for more," I replied. "And brace yourself for a bombardment of hate mail."

That two-year-old article quickly set a new record, with more traffic than the travel magazine had ever received in a single weekend, and more comments on a single article. I reached out to Daphne to correct a minor detail about my time in the country. She replied within moments, and we began a correspondence. It turned out we had mutual friends. I would go on to write several popular guest posts for her site, but back in 2013 I was still there on the sidelines, watching as her frustration turned to fear after the election of Muscat.

Daphne took the measure of Malta's new prime minister straight away. "The annoying only son of doting older parents," she wrote, "who has been accustomed from birth to being the center of attention for adults in whose eyes he could do no wrong, and who admired his every move and word." Muscat had gotten his start in the media empire owned by Mintoff's Labour Party. "He reached his forties in a similar situation, always placing himself in contexts where he would shine, largely because there was no competition. For example, politics in the Labour Party, and journalism at Maltastar and Super One." She dreaded the return of Labour to power and feared that the country would be plunged back into the turmoil her generation had fought so hard to get out of.

Daphne was born in 1964, the year Malta achieved independence, and came of age during the Cold War and the Mintoff regime. In many ways she was a typical middle-class convent-educated girl. The eldest of four daughters of businessman Michael Alfred Vella and Rose Marie Vella, she grew up in the lovely seaside town of Sliema, where she was raised to value decency, honesty, and moral conviction.

Education was an early casualty of Mintoff's fight with the clergy, and the now nineteen-year-old Daphne joined a march in Sliema in 1984 to protest his attempt to close the country's church-run schools.

She was arrested at a peaceful sit-in and charged with assaulting a very large police officer. They took her to the dingy Floriana lockup, where she was strip-searched, held overnight in a filthy cell, and threatened into signing a false confession by an inspector who would go on to become the speaker of the house of parliament.

Her sister Corinne was with her at the time. She described these events for the Tortoise podcast *My Mother's Murder* in February 2020: "When someone was arrested, you didn't know what was going to happen until they came out. The police were something to be feared at the time, not because they were highly disciplined, but as a combination of unmitigated power, total amalgamation with a government that had absolutely no regard for personal rights, and no means of redress." In those years, people emerged from the Floriana jail so badly beaten that they needed to be hospitalized. One man came out in the trunk of a car and was sent straight to the morgue. "You couldn't talk about politics at school because people were afraid that if they spoke up, classmates would go back and report to their parents what you were saying. That meant your parents got into trouble. Your business or your property would be expropriated, for instance, or you'd be seen as an enemy of the state."

Daphne's treatment at the hands of Inspector Anglu Farrugia left an impression that would shape the rest of her life.

"She was a born journalist," her father would say, years later. "She was not the sort of person who would have had certain knowledge and been able to keep it back. I don't think she would have been able to live with herself."

Shy, reserved, and quiet in person, her written voice was direct, witty, and expressed in an impeccable English that put the island's other journalists to shame. In a media landscape where fear of retaliation was the norm, in 1990 she became the first independent political columnist in the country to write under her real name. Until then, no one used bylines, and columns had been written under pen names. Malta's deeply misogynistic society struggled to believe this twenty-five-year-old woman was more than a façade. Readers suspected that her father or her soft-spoken, property lawyer husband was writing it. But she quickly became the country's most widely read columnist, the one whose name appeared on advertisements: "Don't miss Daphne on Sunday."

She started her *Running Commentary* website in 2008. She continued to write a column for the *Malta Independent* and to produce the style magazine *Taste & Flair*, but the internet gave her an outlet that was free of an editor's censoring hand, and free from publishers who lived in fear of losing an advertiser's revenue or receiving a powerful politician's wrath. She called out corruption on both sides of the political spectrum, which earned her enemies, and she mocked bad behavior of high officials and Maltese society with a scathing wit. No one was beyond scrutiny. She never suffered fools, and she hated opportunists, arse kissers, and bootlickers.

Daphne's blog soon outstripped the combined daily readership of the country's main newspapers. She wasn't just influencing the political agenda; she was setting it. Critics complained that *Running Commentary* sometimes verged on a gossip column, with personal attacks tinged with classism. And Daphne could be ruthless when she saw politicians acting like "bogans" or "chavs." But her frustration was born of a sense that Malta could be so much more than it was, if only individuals would raise their own standards and their expectations. She fought hard for what she believed were European values in a nation that still hadn't shaken off its colonial subservience and its pirate past.

As an investigative journalist, she was second to none. She understood the networks of power in Malta, who was related to who, and what roles they had played under previous administrations. And she had sources who trusted her—she called them her "international army of spies." It was impossible for a politician to sneak abroad or hold a meeting on the sly without her finding out about it. I've often wondered if her meticulous approach to investigation came in part from her return to school in the late 1990s as a mature student to pursue a bachelor's degree in archaeology (with honors) from the University of Malta. That gimlet eye also gave her a deep understanding of the strange, insular culture she was immersed in.

Writing the news in such a small place comes with a price. The people you end up reporting about are people you know, or their friends, relatives, and neighbors. In 1994 the family's border collie had its throat slit, and its body was placed across their doorstep. Their front door was doused and set on fire in 1995, a typically anonymous response to criticism. And in 2006 tires were stacked against a glass door at the back of the house, doused in petrol, and set alight in a clear case of attempted murder. The family's death was only averted because the youngest son, Paul, returned home late and found the fire before it engulfed their home.

With Muscat's election, the threats against Daphne took a different form. Libel suits had long been used as weaponized reputation management in Malta, with cases being taken out against journalists to silence a story or intimidate others from writing. Like many others, Daphne was sued, some fifteen times between 1989 and 2012. But from the election of Muscat onward, she was sued fifty-one times, always by a government or Labour Party official. Her demonization in Labour Party media also turned to open hatred when enraged supporters spotted her walking in Rabat in 2013 and chased her down the street. She was forced to take shelter in a nearby convent until the police arrived, as the mob—among them the Labour mayor of Zurrieq, Ignatius Farrugia—stood outside baying for blood.

They were chanting, "We have power now! Muscat is our leader!"

# PARTIES
# IN SEPARATE ROOMS

As much as I loved living in that cavernous old house in Zejtun, I'd begun to think of downsizing to something cheaper when Marian told us the palazzo was for sale.

We decided to hold a sort of reverse housewarming, to say goodbye to a place we'd loved and that held so many memories, some good and some sad. Tomoko loaded the dining room table with carefully prepared plates of Japanese food, and I loaded the cellar with wines and other munitions of peace. We opened our heavy wooden door to some of the friends we'd made in our first island years: an elderly man from Naxxar whose father had been in the military uniform trade during the British period; a fellow desert enthusiast I'd met in the Sahara, who spent his evenings poring over satellite images in search of prehistoric stone circles; a photographer and his family who lived in an old stone house around the corner; and, of course, Dr. Dalli. The last stragglers didn't leave until 4 a.m., just as the sun was peeking its confused morning face over the horizon.

The next evening we stopped by our favorite pizza place around the corner for one last meal. Sammy, the owner, was the hardest working man in Malta. After posing for photos with both of us, individually and collectively, he handed Tomoko two pizzas and a bunch of beers and refused to take any money. We had a similar response when we said goodbye to the vegetable vendor, a young couple who sourced their produce direct from local farms. And the lady at the bakery on the corner came out from behind the counter to hug and kiss Tomoko, though she'd never displayed much friendliness when we'd stopped to buy a *pastizzi* or a slice of cake. It felt like the village had opened up to us with kindness just as we were turning our backs on it. But the house was for sale, and we had to go.

In late 2013 we moved to a penthouse high on a hill on the outskirts of Mosta, where we would have the entire top floor. I had initial misgivings about living in an apartment, but there would be no stomping neighbors above us and no blaring television seeping through shared walls.

"You will find it easy to work here," Sofija, our landlord, said when we signed the contract. "*Mela*, it's so quiet. I stayed here two years. There was just me and the guy in the ground floor maisonette."

Buildings made of stone do not creak. There is no wood to announce one's squeaking midnight entrance, only the silent glide of stocking feet on ceramic tiles. Drop a euro coin in the parking garage and you will hear it in the penthouse and find yourself patting your pockets, checking for holes. The clack of high-heeled shoes two floors below at 6 a.m. pierced stone with a clarity the carrying power of which could only be exceeded by one other instrument: the human voice.

"Euuuuh!" echoed through the light well at the back of the apartment and drew me to my study the day after we moved in. It was answered by a similar "Euuuuh!" from somewhere farther down.

I approached the window from an oblique angle and edged out past the sill. The woman on the third floor was grunting at her sister in the ground floor maisonette. And then a string was lowered with a cleaning bucket tied to the end. The maisonette sister dropped in a loaf of bread and what looked like a jar of Nescafé, and it was hauled back up. This swapping of items by way of the bucket was a regular occurrence. The light well also served as an amplifier for long private conversations, a sort of proto-can-and-string telephone. I suppose it was better than walking down the stairs or spending credits on a phone call.

Maltese houses had names, like Starlight or Diamond Bite or even Immaculate Conception, which always made me think of a pool of clotting sperm. Religious imagery aside, the more grandiose the name, the shabbier the dwelling. Which didn't say much for our decision to move into a building called LUXE Mansions. We should have expected the shabbiness we got: surface polish and subsurface rot.

LUXE Mansions would be under construction for the entire two and a half years we lived there. Some apartment was always being fixed up, or plumbing being installed, or holes being drilled in walls for electrical wiring.

Semiprofessional builders in Malta took a Battle of the Somme approach: long periods of silence followed by bursts of violent drilling that always commenced at dawn. They invariably insisted on showing up at 6 or 7 a.m. and worked for half an hour before packing up and going home.

It was like waking up inside an immense tooth as a determined dentist had a go. Drills vibrated through the walls like a tuning fork, until my head began to resonate, and finally my bones. When it stopped, our rooms filled with a faint scent of limestone dust. The tether of sanity slipped a little looser, receding with the ability to form coherent thoughts. Each time we went out, we had to hopscotch over an enormous Medusa's hair of extension cords that the contractors ran from the apartment they were working on to the power plug in the electrical room. They were freeloading electricity from the building's common area, so we not only suffered from this noise, we had the

privilege of splitting the bill for it too. Packaging materials, broken
plaster, cardboard, and dirt were strewn all over the lobby and stairs.
They simply dropped it on the ground and walked away as though
they didn't see it once they'd cast it aside. These campaigns would last
about a week, and then an uneasy silence would descend for a month.
It took years to fix up a small shell apartment enough to move in.

Of course, nothing was ever truly fixed; it was just temporarily not
broken. We had no hot water in our kitchen because the heater had
been installed incorrectly and the wiring burned out in the rain. The
water pressure pump on the roof broke, leaving us without hot water
for a week in winter. The front door lock seized up and fell apart. And
the lift was completely out of commission six times. Once I became
trapped inside when it broke down between floors. I had to pry open
the door and climb out because the emergency button was never connected and no one would answer my call.

Construction was driving the Labour Party's economic boom, so
it was the building that mattered, not the finishing. Muscat dreamed
of transforming the island into "Dubai in the Mediterranean," and he
didn't care how much of the overcrowded country's remaining green
space had to be sacrificed to those with the right political connections.
Nonstop construction became the reality in every village as the new
prime minister formed an alliance with the Malta Developers Association. Hideous high-rise towers were proposed in the center of what
used to be peaceful seaside villages, where their physical structure
would cast nearly as much shade as the rumors of money laundering
that surrounded them. Cheap blocks of flats spread across terraced
fields like some crusty limestone impetigo. Excavators perched peril-
ously at the edges of cliffs or were lifted onto rooftops that couldn't
possibly support their weight. Plasterers dangled from windows by
one hand and coated a wall with the other. Mobile cranes tipped over

with monotonous regularity, blocking streets and knocking down walls like siege engines from the time of the knights.

Malta Developers Association president Sandro Chetcuti and the Concrete Kings had publicly vowed to "make hay while the sun shines." It was the start of the construction boom, which would transform the visual landscape of the tiny island irreparably. What was once the jewel of the Mediterranean was becoming a characterless urban slum.

Without distinct seasons, every day was the same. I knew each morning when I woke up that it would be sunny and hot, and that today would be just like the day before. The calendar was arbitrary. There was nothing to mark the passing of time. No weekends for the self-employed. No orderly procession. No sense of the sands running out. If I didn't get something done, there was always tomorrow. "Don't worry," my neighbor said. "Take a nap." And that's what everyone did. Flooded roads were forgotten the moment the rain stopped. Things that fell apart were temporarily patched. Anything looming beyond tomorrow existed in a future that never took shape.

The social calendar offered no solace to a life lived outside of time. I'd already begun to dread those claustrophobic expat gatherings where most of the attendees showed up for free wine, and where exactly the same griping conversations took place with exactly the same people again and again. I was more interested in the elderly Maltese men and women we'd met who had experienced life under the British, lived through the Mintoff years, and seen how far their country had come. They were watching the effort of generations going up in flames, along with everything that was great about their childhood, as the young were swept up in a wave of temporary prosperity and easy money and the bubble-dwelling expats looked away.

As the melancholy introspection and false camaraderie of another
New Year's Eve approached, we were invited to a party across the
island, hosted by a British businessman, to ring in 2015. I was determined to have a bad time. Always one to look for the best in every
situation despite my pessimism, Tomoko was equally determined
to ignore me. If it hadn't been for her outgoing nature and growing
professional network, we would have stopped going anywhere at all.
Their street was marked by a wrought-iron sign set in a triangular
island in the center of the road. "Victoria Gardens," I said, reading
aloud. "Such a grandiose name for that patch of scrub grass, dog shit,
and broken bottles."

"Look, if you didn't want to come, you could just stay home."

"On the contrary, I wouldn't miss it. Besides, it could be worse.
There's always the 'entertainment district.' Abandoned Burger King
containers and vomit slicks. Paceville has more vomit per square
meter than a maternity ward. Did you know that?"

I'm pretty sure she did know that, but our arrival cut short her
reply.

I rang the bell with grim determination. The lady who opened the
door was so caked with makeup she looked like she'd come from a
coffin fitting. "Awwwl-right?" she said, ushering us in with a cracked
plaster smile.

The room was a shining glaze of marble floors, gleaming tiles, and
hard overstuffed furniture that looked expensive but probably wasn't.
All of this was bracketed by an astonishing clutter of useless objects
meant, I suppose, as a display of wealth. We passed the owner of the
house on our way through. He was giving a neighbor the grand tour.

"Did you notice my enormous TV? It's over there. Take a look at
that TV." It was the largest object in a living room where I noted a
conspicuous absence of books.

We soon located some people we knew, deep in the bowels of the vast hillside house. Maltese and foreigners had segregated themselves in separate rooms, each absorbed in their own conversational worlds, polite but unmixed. We only met at the buffet table, laden with home-cooked delicacies, cheese platters, canapés, and sweets, including the usual two or three dishes of doubtful provenance.

The evening passed in a blur of shouting, with lashings of wine that ranged from poor to mediocre, with the occasional drinkable glass. I watched an old Maltese man tear a banana from the host's own fruit bowl and slide it down his throat like a sword swallower. "Nothing like a good wholesome ba-naa-naaaa," he said, before turning on the expat next to him, prodding him in the chest with a stubby finger, and ranting about the abuses of British colonialism.

As I edged past them, I heard the other man say, "Well, the British have been gone for forty years. What have you done since to fix your own problems?"

"Know what you can do, sir? Go back to your country! We never asked you to come here."

"You did, actually," the Brit replied. "You begged us to come and kick out the French."

I met the eyes of another expat who was also slipping away from the fray. "What's with that guy?" I said. "Why's he so angry?"

"You haven't been here very long, mate. They're only going to re-main friendly and helpful as long as they can take advantage of you one way or another."

His opinion didn't match my feelings about the small circle of older friends I'd formed in our quiet village life. "But what about 'plucky little Malta, defying the odds'?" I asked. The island's heroism and Peter's war stories remained etched in my memory.

A local journalist heard me and cut in. "Half-truths," she said. "We didn't have a choice. If the Nazis had invaded Malta, 90 percent of the Maltese would have rushed to collaborate. The George Cross was

won by the very few in the name of the many who would have fled if
they could."

I wanted to argue the point, but we were beset by a god-awful roar
from somewhere below, as the house shook with the sound of a thousand angry bees attacking in unison.

"Oh, that's Neville," an older lady said, referring to the homeown-
er's son. "Have you seen his car? You must see the Car." Neville had
descended to the underground garage, glassed in next to the main
basement room, where he fired up his conspicuously parked Porsche
and made sure everyone knew it was there by racing the engine for at
least fifteen minutes.

It might seem like freedom to move to a Mediterranean island of
near-constant sunshine, near-absent responsibility, and nothing to
do but nibble olives and sip wine, or perhaps go for a sail. But the
more I encountered these retired expats with their cyclical lives, the
more it began to look like a sham freedom made up of bored and
lonely people living in small, uncomfortable stone houses in a remote
backwater. They hadn't just retired from work. They had retired from
the world.

Another expat friend sympathized with my frustrations but explained why he was content to remain. "I like my life here," he said.
"It's easy. I live by the water. Swim every day. My gym is down the
street. Lots of friends here. I guess I'm not hard to please."

I asked a Calabrian who had relocated to the island after marrying
a Maltese girl if he found it difficult to fit in. He brought the tips
of his fingers together and moved his hand up and down. "They put
ricotta in the lasagna," he said. And because I didn't react with suffi-
cient gravity to this abomination, he said it again more slowly.

The only thing we didn't discuss at the party was local politics.
Expats were strangely detached from the scandals. I don't know if
they were afraid to voice an opinion, given the inevitable backlash,

or if they really didn't smell the stench that seemed to be filling the room. They simply avoided talking about it—at least until it became so surreal that pretending it away was no longer an option.

Back home, I took one last nightcap on the roof before turning in.

"That's odd," I said, looking toward Sicily, where the approach lights of a large jet had just come on. "There shouldn't be any flights arriving this late."

We lived directly beneath the flight path of the airport. The passenger jets were still a couple thousand feet up when they passed over our building, but standing on our penthouse terrace you'd swear they were going to skim the roof.

When the plane passed over, it was painted solid white, with four engines, but I couldn't see any markings apart from a tail number. I ducked inside to grab my iPad and activated the Flight Tracker app. I could still see blinking wing lights in the distance when I came back out. It hadn't quite reached the runway.

"It doesn't show up at all…"

"Well, maybe they missed that one," Tomoko said.

"Even planes with no information show up on here. They say 'private jet' or 'government' or 'military.' Sometimes they won't tell you the flight plan, just where it originated. But that plane is missing. It's like it doesn't exist."

I was finally beginning to understand that nothing in Malta was ever as it appeared. Families and villages had their own dark secrets. Political graft took place just out of sight. Smugglers of drugs, cigarettes, pilfered fuel, and people operated in plain sight from docks in Marsa, right on Valletta's Grand Harbour. And shadowy intelligence agencies and offshore businesses did their thing behind blank walls and unmarked doors.

We'd watched on the news as Malta's former patron, Muammar

Gaddafi, was sodomized with a bayonet before being beaten and then shot to death in the street by his own people in October 2011. What began as a Libyan insurrection was now a full-blown civil war. The embers of the Arab Spring were still smoldering too, and the war in Syria was now at full blaze.

Those unmarked 3 a.m. flights continued throughout the summer. When fighter jets arrived by day, the newspaper published immediate denials without being asked: "Three Tornado jets arrived from Britain today to refuel. They were on a training flight. It doesn't have anything to do with Libya." The Russians were active too, and the Chinese were spreading their tentacles by stealth, opening a cultural center, pushing quietly to get the Chinese language taught in schools, and smiling and nodding as they slipped in deeper.

# IT WAS A BLIND
# AND BROKEN TIME

The endless daily litany of corruption scandals and strange crimes that formed the backdrop to our first four island years hadn't traveled farther than the local news, but the country began its descent to international infamy in March 2016 when 11.5 million confidential documents from Panamanian law firm Mossack Fonseca were leaked to the German newspaper *Süddeutsche Zeitung*.

The yearlong Panama Papers investigation by the International Consortium of Investigative Journalists shone a light on the secret world of legal tax-avoidance structures used by wealthy individuals to move and hide money. Dozens of politicians were named in the leak, including current and former world leaders as well as public officials, celebrities, and businesspeople, but only one European Union member state had a sitting government minister on the list.

Europeans were shocked to learn that Joseph Muscat's star cabinet minister Konrad Mizzi had set up a secret Panama company structure and offshore trust within seventy-two hours of the Labour Party's election—and he wasn't the only member of the government to be named.

The Panamanian firm was represented in Malta by NexiaBT, an accounting company run by Brian Tonna. Tonna wasn't a big player

before the election, but when Muscat took power, island rumor said
the accountant was given a desk at the Auberge de Castille, right
down the hall from the prime minister. Whether or not that detail
proved true, the previously unknown firm would rake in €2.4 million
in government contracts during the first four years alone, 85 percent
of it through direct orders for everything from negotiations on a controversial public-private hospital deal to a study on public toilets.

NexiaBT opened two other anonymous Panama shell companies
at the same time as they set one up for Mizzi called Hearnville. A
company called Tillgate belonged to the prime minister's chief of
staff, Keith Schembri. And Tonna's partner, Karl Cini, told Mossack
Fonseca that the ultimate beneficial owner of the third company,
Egrant, "will be an individual and I will speak to Luis [a Mossack
Fonseca employee] on Skype to give him more details." No one was
taking any chances with that name. But who could be more sensitive
than the chief of staff, second most powerful man in the country?

Large black bags of shredded paper appeared outside the accountant's San Ġwann office days after the story broke. They were collected
by trucks from Kasco, a paper company owned by Keith Schembri. It
wouldn't be the only time bags of shredded paper followed some new
revelation published by Daphne Caruana Galizia.

As protests raged across the island, Mizzi admitted to having
opened the company but continued to deny he'd done anything
wrong. "The trust was set up for long-term family asset management
and inheritance," he said.

He didn't have any known assets to protect, apart from a rundown
row house in a distant suburb of London, and when he incorporated
his company, he'd ticked a box that confirmed he wouldn't be using
it to manage an inheritance. "I have always been and will always be
transparent in my state of affairs," he said. He'd also ticked boxes
marked "No audit" and "Total secrecy and confidentiality."

Mizzi's most outrageous excuse was that his Panama company never had a bank account, prompting newspaper columnists to compare him to a burglar in one's living room who might say, "Yes, okay, I broke in, but I haven't stolen anything yet." It wasn't for lack of trying. NexiaBT had attempted to open accounts for all three companies in nine different jurisdictions. No one would touch them when they realized they were dealing with politically exposed persons. In summing up their efforts, Daphne wrote, "It shows that two jurisdictions which are hardly noted for tough laws [against money laundering] considered them to be too high-risk."

At the point where the email chain breaks off, their focus had shifted to Dubai—a popular travel destination for Maltese politicians, including Mizzi and Muscat. But why struggle to open a foreign account when you have the power to license your own bank? Enter Ali Sadr Hasheminejad, a thirty-four-year-old Iranian with no prior banking experience. He applied for a banking license in Malta in October 2013, and it was granted three months later. No one seemed to inquire too deeply into where his startup funding came from.

So what was Mizzi up to? Incoming funds for the three Panama companies were listed as originating from "brokerage fees" and "a waste management business." They expected to receive €5,000 per day from two target clients, 17 Black and Macbridge, with business activities to include infrastructure projects, recycling, remote gaming, fisheries, maritime projects, and tourism.

Cini from NexiaBT stressed again that the beneficial owners were to be concealed. "The companies will act as a vehicle of [sic] extracting the profits from this venture," he wrote, "since from a commercially sensitive perspective they cannot appear as direct shareholders, either personally or via holding entities." Brokerage fees are a common euphemism for bribes or kickbacks.

When the prime minister finally called a press conference in late

April, he was expected to announce the dismissal of his embattled minister and his chief of staff. Instead, he defended them. "The Panama Papers affair hurts us, personally and politically," he said, "and even if nothing illegal has happened, better behavior is expected." The "politically naïve" Mizzi would be stripped of the health and energy portfolios but would remain in the cabinet, where he was to serve in some unspecified role directly under Muscat himself as minister in the Office of the Prime Minister.

As for Schembri, he would remain as chief of staff. "He is not a political figure," Muscat said, referring to the fact that the businessman had been appointed rather than elected. "I trust him." The prime minister would of course dismiss these men if an independent tax audit of their overseas finances found they'd broken any laws, but that process was expected to take some time.

Anyone familiar with offshore shell companies knew an audit would only examine documents submitted by the subject of the inquiry. But Muscat's excuse was directed at Labour supporters whose faith in their king had briefly been shaken. They needed an empty catchphrase for village arguments, and the reassurance that anyone who didn't accept "wait for the audit" was part of a Nationalist plot to take power.

The Financial Intelligence Analysis Unit (FIAU), Malta's money-laundering watchdog, wasn't convinced. Testifying years later before a public inquiry in 2020, then-head Manfred Galdes said, "We felt the information was sufficiently serious to be passed on to the police without delay." He hand-delivered the report of his investigation to Police Commissioner Michael Cassar because he didn't trust anyone with it, not even a messenger. The FIAU head expected to see immediate orders to freeze bank accounts, but the police commissioner took one look at what had landed in his lap and went on sick leave.

He resigned days later, to be replaced by Lawrence Cutajar, a football fanboy who had praised the prime minister's brass balls on Facebook. The new police commissioner shoved the reports on Mizzi and Schembri deep in a drawer to collect dust, and when Galdes saw this, he resigned too. He never made his reasons public, but those following the case concluded that the former FIAU head had refused to whitewash what looked an awful lot like financial crimes.

Nothing about the Panama Papers was speculation. The leaks contained entire email chains, account opening forms, and even scans of personal documents like passports and bank reference letters. They caused the resignation of the prime minister of Iceland, the Ukrainian prime minister, and a Spanish industrial minister and sparked angry protests around the globe. But while the authorities in eighty-two countries were busy digging into these shocking revelations, the police in Malta saw no reasonable suspicion to carry out an investigation. In a normal country, people would go to jail for what in Malta was met with a shrug.

Part of it may have been a question of language. Daphne pointed out that Maltese used the English word "commission" for a cut of any kind. "It doesn't have a word for an illicit cut," she said, "because in Maltese culture, anyone can take a cut from anything, and it is their 'right.' There's absolutely no awareness that some cuts are completely illegal, by their very nature, and especially when you are a politician."

Only journalists affiliated with the International Consortium of Investigative Journalists had access to the Panama Papers, and Muscat's inner circle didn't know how much dirt the data leak contained.

Why was Joseph Muscat so determined to protect Mizzi and Schembri, despite the obvious political damage that could have been avoided by cutting them loose? And who owned Egrant, the mysterious third company set up within days of the election that brought this government to power?

The prime minister made a performance of calling for magisterial inquiries, implying that what was really just the collection and preservation of evidence was in fact a criminal investigation. The process would drag on for years as each of the main players—backed by the government—did everything they could to stall those inquiries, hiding out in a strange gray area between accusation and legal conviction, proclaiming themselves innocent because they hadn't yet been charged. And then they doubled down on their attacks.

For Labour supporters, Muscat and his party were the government. The laws of the land were less important than a large electoral victory, which in their eyes empowered the majority to impose its will on everyone else. Economy Minister Chris Cardona set the tone in his speech at the Labour Party's 2016 annual general meeting, where he strode across the stage and shouted, "We will take an axe to those who knife us." He was given a standing ovation.

Weeks before the Panama Papers story broke, Daphne had posted a series of blogs that exposed the New Zealand trusts owned by Mizzi and Schembri, the ones created to hold their Panama shell companies. Only the players involved would have understood the subtext and realized she knew so much more.

The government hit back by starting a counterblog run by a semiliterate Muscat crony who targeted Daphne directly, posting photos of her going about her daily business, mocking her, and encouraging commenters to do the same. The blog was written on government pay, from a desk at the Office of the Prime Minister. None of Labour's elected officials thought it odd that the full weight of the state was being directed against a single journalist in a European Union country.

"You would expect a Bolivian peasant or a gutter supporter of the Malta Labour Party not to know why an aide to the head of the government should not be intimidating and assaulting critics of that government, with his boss's full approval, encouragement and backing (and payment)," Daphne wrote. "But there is no way on earth that the Prime Minister and his aide Glenn Bedingfield do not know that this is Third World dictatorship behavior."

The Labour Party also operated secret and closed social media hate groups that worked to dehumanize Daphne while spreading a unified counternarrative to the scandals she exposed, filling the heads of their followers with incoherent rebuttals, whataboutism, and denial while stoking the fires of their rage. In a country where political party support resembled the passionate advocacy of football hooligans for their local club, these tactics worked so well that masses of followers who had never read Daphne's writing—who in many cases couldn't even read English—loathed her with the passion of medieval witch burners. Party minions called her the Queen of Bile, "that blogger," and a troll; they couldn't bear to utter her name. As a woman writing in the misogynist southern Mediterranean, she was also called aggressive, hysterical, and hormonal—especially by the furious undersized men whose dirty dealing she exposed.

But the greatest threat to rationality was monopolistic control of the media. Malta's situation is unique in Europe, with the two main political parties owning their own television and radio stations, and both daily and weekly print media. There was no independent source for television news; Net and ONE were directly owned by the Nationalist and Labour Parties, respectively. Television news was broadcast entirely in Maltese, and the few independent news outlets published in English. The Public Broadcasting Service—an outlet with a constitutional obligation to be strictly impartial—had, in effect, become a branch of ONE, reporting the same biased Labour Party line and underreporting or completely avoiding exactly the same inconvenient truths.

Most of the relentless propaganda unleashed by the government was aimed at its own supporters, who lived in a largely monolingual world where the party was always right. And lest anyone attempt to think for themselves, independent print and online news sources were tarred as "negative," biased, or "traitors to Malta."

Journalists and media outlets that weren't directly controlled by Labour could allegedly be influenced—like *Malta Today*, whose founder and co-owner was the recipient of large government advertising contracts, and who would be exposed as having taken midnight phone calls from Schembri prior to releasing stories aimed at discrediting major revelations by Daphne. The rest could be intimidated with libel suits, social censure, withheld advertising, and physical threats. Punitive libel suits were routinely filed on a whim in Malta, forcing the defendant into years of expensive legal wrangling, only to drop the case before resolution lest the plaintiff's testimony incriminate themselves. A libel case also gave politicians an excuse for avoiding comment. "This is the standard response of the cornered Maltese politician, particularly in sex-and-corruption cases," Daphne wrote. "Suing for libel, or just announcing that you are, is a way of dealing with the immediate pressure of public opinion and your political bosses. Sue for libel—and then we'll see." And so they kicked their excuses down the road, to a time when the outrage had cooled and everyone had forgotten about the scandal. But journalists couldn't afford to ignore these expensive evasions. Failure to respond meant concession and the payment of penalties. It was easier not to write about controversial topics at all.

Daphne would not be intimidated, so she was targeted. Mizzi tried using the courts to force her to reveal her sources by claiming she wasn't a journalist, but the judiciary hadn't yet been fully compromised and the judge denied his request, referring to a European

Court of Human Rights verdict in which the protection of sources was described as "one of the basic conditions for press freedom."

High-priced London lawyers working for Henley & Partners, concessionaire of the country's citizenship-by-investment program, raised the stakes by threatening Daphne and other Maltese media houses with financially ruinous international lawsuits over stories they had published about the controversial scheme. The newspapers caved in and removed their stories, but Daphne published Henley's emails—and their lawyers' letters—in full.

It later transpired that Henley & Partners had sought the government's permission to intimidate her in this way, and if that wasn't possible, to bankrupt her. The firm's chairman, Christian Kaelin, had sent the email to "Keith, Joseph" at their respective @josephmuscat .com email addresses, which they had been using to conduct official business via private servers, rather than their official government addresses. The prime minister of Malta replied, "i don't object," and Schembri said, "Thanks, Chris. This looks good. Very kind regards."

But it was the "axe man," Chris Cardona, who took this tried-and-true tactic to new extremes. When Daphne reported that the economy minister had been seen having a threesome in a brothel with his aide while they were in Germany on European Union business, the minister tried bankrupting her into submission with libel suits and an unprecedented garnishee order that froze her accounts to the amount of €46,000. When word got out, *Running Commentary* readers, led by the popular radio host David Thake, raised €70,000 in thirty-six hours through a crowdfunding campaign to match the frozen funds. Minister Cardona's bluster turned to scurrying when Daphne subpoenaed his mobile phone records, which would prove whether he was in his hotel room raiding the minibar as he claimed or engaging sex workers on government time.

Labour support soared to new heights as the behavior of those in power sunk to new depths. As long as they controlled the institutions, they were untouchable. But underneath their collective rage was a hard core of cowardice. They were afraid of Daphne because she wasn't afraid of them, and she couldn't be bought.

# BOOKS JUST FURNISH
# A ROOM

Our two-year penthouse residency came to an end in spring 2015 when Sofija flaked out.

"Has some rental agent been hounding you?" I asked, covering one ear to block out the drilling and shouting from below.

"It's the uncertainty," she said. "I need to know what you're planning to do."

"Sofija, I told you. We're not sure if we'll stay in Malta much longer, but we're not going to pull a runner. I know that happens a lot, but where I come from it's expected to give two months' notice."

"Yes yes yes," she said. "We already extended by six months." I heard her swallow once and take a deep breath as she built up to whatever it was she wanted to say. "I need you to commit to two years."

"There's no way I can commit to two years. We could talk about a year, but two is too far ahead."

"That agent is calling me constantly," she said. "I have to give her an answer. There's an Italian lady who wants the place—"

"Look, Sofija, I can't give you an answer today. Tomoko's in Japan visiting her family—"

"I need you to sign for two years," she repeated. "And I need to know right now."

I spoke to my wife later that day. "We have to move again."

"Wasn't there a phantom Italian lady with Marian, too?"

When we were negotiating for the palazzo, the agent had told us there was an Italian friend in the picture who wanted the house so badly but the owner seemed to prefer us. She used this mysterious stranger to drive up the price by another hundred a month. I wanted to live there, so I agreed. But the penthouse had been nothing but problems right from the start, and it wasn't worth what Sofija was asking.

Our move from the Palazzo Marija to the penthouse had gone as smoothly as possible, but leaving was more of a challenge. We decided to downsize again, to find a flat where we could both have studies to work in and spend more time abroad. We couldn't justify being away so much when we were renting a palazzo, but a small apartment in a remote village was still a very cheap European base.

After a strange and exasperating search involving multiple half-finished apartments, including one with a tiki bar and a shattered toilet in the hall, a detective who moonlighted as a realtor found us a place on the outskirts of Zurrieq, one of the oldest villages in the island's south. It was a typical Maltese townhouse on a dead-end street. The front window overlooked terraced fields with dry stone walls and the deep seaside cleft of the Blue Grotto, with a view all the way to Mdina and Dingli radar station. Our landlord, Carmen, lived upstairs, with an entrance on a different street. The flat belonged to a daughter who had immigrated to Australia years before. It was clean and simple and very cheap, and with only Carmen living above, it promised to be quiet. Carmen saw me at my desk many times, but nearly a year would pass before she asked me what I did for a living. I said that I was a writer.

She pointed at the wall behind me, where six large bookcases were stuffed with volumes of all kinds. "Did you write all of them?"

"No," I said. "Just the one." I held up a paperback copy of my first book. "It took ten years."

"Ten years! What a waste of time. You can't make money from that."

In the two years we lived there she never asked me about my work again. She never remarked on the books she passed on the coffee table either—and I tested her by leaving out a book on atheism called *God Is Not Great* and another called *Child-Free and Loving It!* But despite Carmen's lack of curiosity, that conversation about books wasn't the end of it. Tomoko went to the vegetable vendor on the corner two weeks later to buy some produce. After attempting to teach her the Maltese names of several items, the vendor set down his basket and leaned on the counter.

"Your husband is a very intelligent man," he said, tapping the side of his head. "Veeeeery intelligent." Tomoko must have looked surprised at this, because he raised a finger and added, "I know. Carmen told me."

I had never met this man and had never ventured into his shop. I didn't know anyone at all in our neighborhood. But I was perceived as intelligent simply due to book ownership. I joked that I'd either be revered as a sage or burned as a witch, and I wasn't sure yet which way it would go.

Why did people in the village assume I was intelligent simply because they thought I read books? I suppose it's because readers are mysterious. They're too quiet. You don't know what they're thinking, and they like to spend time alone. To read in Malta was also unusual. Homes without a bookshelf—and with no books at all—were the norm in the country with the European Union's lowest rate of reading. In November 2013 the *Times of Malta* reported that 44 percent of Maltese had not read a book in the last twelve months.

"Look around a hospital waiting room," my artist friend Becks told me. "The only people reading a book are foreigners. Books are for school and exams—that's our mentality. The only book I ever saw in the hands of people who never read was *Fifty Shades of Grey*."

The people I met on the island were among the least curious I'd ever encountered; their thirst for information seemed to stop at the immediate borders of their lives. Part of this could be attributed to the influence of the family. Language skills develop on the back of curiosity and a hunger for knowledge. Without a rich vocabulary to describe your ideas, you end up using the ideas of others. Such people don't just speak in clichés, they think in them too. And when your only proficiency is a language so few people speak, then language too becomes an island.

The quality of education was also to blame. In November 2015 the *Times of Malta* reported on the results of the latest secondary education certificate examinations in history. A total of 205 students applied for the exam, and 54 percent managed a passing mark. Another third did so badly their grade couldn't be classified, and ten applicants didn't bother to show up. Despite the devastating impact of World War II on Malta—which was felt by the grandparents of these very same students—many were unable to say who Winston Churchill was. They were also unable to explain the term Iron Curtain or the division of Europe into two opposing blocs, and only a couple of candidates were able to explain the Marshall Plan.

The roots of this cultural ignorance were deep. Anthropologist Jeremy Boissevain said in a press interview, "It's all part of a hierarchy, in which authority doesn't want to be questioned. Government doesn't like being questioned, the church doesn't like being questioned, fathers don't like being questioned by their children, and men don't want to be questioned by women."

"You'll find this interesting," Tomoko said one afternoon as she walked into my study and dropped two documents on my desk. They were examination booklets from the University of Malta, one in history and one in English literature.

"Where did you get these?"

"It doesn't matter. But have a look through them."

Rote memorization. Multiple choice. Two-line answers. At first glance I thought they were basic high school tests. That was the standard, according to Becks. "Today's university students don't care about anything except lack of parking on campus and their stipends. Lectures are treated as lessons. The teacher talks and the students take it down verbatim, unquestioningly, so they can vomit it back for the final. Are we going to be tested on this? If not, it isn't important."

Another Maltese friend pursuing a master's degree in the United Kingdom provided further confirmation that original thought was simply not part of the curriculum. She'd earned undergraduate and graduate degrees in science from the University of Malta, but when I asked her how her new course was going, she said she was struggling. "I've never had to write a thesis before," she told me, "or to formulate a research problem."

Responsibility for the deterioration of higher education can be laid at the feet of Dom Mintoff. While the fiery Labour leader initially made efforts to modernize the university by hiring Ralf Dahrendorf (director of the London School of Economics) and John Horlock (vice chancellor of the University of Salford), a visit to Mao's China on his round-the-world begging-bowl tour had left Mintoff with a profound impression of the power of the one-party state. The increasingly autocratic leader realized that power in such countries rested on the suppression of the educated, so he established il-Brigata, his cut-rate children's version of Mao's Red Guard. He also slashed the university's funds, deliberately left key positions vacant, and instituted a student-worker scheme where students alternated six months

of study and six months of work—a situation that, said Dahrendorf
to Mintoff in a 1978 letter, "produces either unhappy workers or
under-qualified students, or both. It adds nothing to education or to
social integration." When violent thugs intimidated both staff and
students, police protected the bullies. Dahrendorf would eventually
resign from his post, lamenting in his resignation letter that "only a
ruin of a university remains."

The educational legacy of Mintoff did much to ensure Joseph
Muscat's victory and his continued hegemony despite wave after wave
of scandals. Labour's support was strongest among the most poorly
educated (60.8 percent, according to a *Malta Today* survey) and lowest among the most highly educated (24.7 percent).

Daphne Caruana Galizia pointed out where this lack of critical
thinking ability leads. "One of the things I find most disturbing about
Maltese society," she wrote on her blog, "is that the concept of consequences arising from choices and actions is largely alien. People seem
unable to link chains of events to an initial choice, action or decision.
Instead they think in terms of 'mistakes,' to which the consequences
are not linked, and which they do not even regard as consequences
but merely as random events unconnected to others. This is the national disease of fatalism: when it is the Fates who decide, you are not
responsible for the outcome, even if the choice was your own."


Life went on despite the daily corruption scandals, but it became
stranger and stranger. A small airplane crashed on takeoff one summer morning while we were abroad. We saw it on the foreign news,
tilting sharply on its side over the runway and then nosediving into
the ground and exploding in a massive fireball. The twin-turboprop
Fairchild Metroliner Mark III was registered in the United States to
CAE Aviation, a Luxembourg-based company, and it was packed
with electronic surveillance equipment.

The government's first statement in the immediate aftermath was that the plane had been part of a French customs operation monitoring smuggling routes, drugs, and human trafficking from Libya, and that officials from Frontex, the European Union's border control agency, were aboard. But Frontex issued an immediate denial: "The plane that crashed this morning in Malta was not deployed in operational activities coordinated by Frontex. No Frontex staff was onboard." The European commissioner for foreign affairs, Federica Mogherini, also issued a statement saying that there were no European Union officials onboard and that the flight was not related to a European Union activity. But Joseph Muscat insisted that his initial statement was correct. "They were customs officials," he said, "because that's what they told us."

He was soon contradicted by an official statement from French defense minister Jean-Yves Le Drian, who said that French Defense Ministry officials from the General Directorate for External Security and two private contractors were on the plane. It is normal practice in aviation disasters to release the victims' names after families have been informed, but the names of these passengers were not revealed. A team of French investigators arrived on the scene, briefly examined the wreckage, and then loaded it onto a truck and carried it away, and nothing was heard about it again. The General Directorate for External Security is France's external intelligence agency, their CIA.

A few days later the French newspaper *Libération* quoted a Malta-based Libya specialist who said, "Malta is the rear base of all Libyan operations. This is the Casablanca of the 1940s. The French, British, Italians, Americans...everyone is there." The newspaper also pointed out that Malta was the seat of the Libyan Central Bank and the National Oil Company. "It has become the hub of all traffic related to Libya."

At the time of the plane crash, the Gaddafi fortune was sitting in the Bank of Valletta—some €90 million, moved in and out of Malta through Capital Resources Ltd., a Maltese-registered shell company whose sole shareholder was Gaddafi's son Mutassim. The company was run on his behalf by ex–Labour Party treasurer Joseph Sammut. When Mutassim Gaddafi was killed, at age thirty-six, the Libyan press reported that two Bank of Valletta Visa cards were found in his wallet. His heirs have been trying to claim this money ever since, as has the current government of Libya.

I asked Joseph Fitsakis, a specialist in intelligence and national security studies at Coastal Carolina University, for his opinion of the situation. "Malta is very much like other places in the Mediterranean, which are very close to the unstable regions of North Africa and the Middle East yet are themselves relatively safe, as well as politically and economically stable," he said. "It offers intelligence operatives proximity to their target regions, while at the same time ensuring a relative degree of safety in meeting assets, setting up safe houses, communications hubs, etc."

"Do you think the government is aware of these operations?" I asked. "The prime minister's reply to the plane crash made it sound like he had no idea what foreign governments were doing in his country." Given Malta's propensity for dealing with both sides, I could see why they wouldn't trust him.

"I would venture to speculate that the government of Malta knows some of what goes on on the island," Fitsakis replied. "However, there are many competing interests active in Malta, and have been for a long time. I would imagine, therefore, that there are several so called 'unilateral' intelligence operations taking place on the island. These are intelligence operations that the host country has not consented to."

Some of those competing interests were private. Toward the end of our time on the island, Maltese arms dealer James Fenech would be charged with breaching European Union sanctions when he supplied military-grade rigid-hull inflatable boats for a bungled mercenary operation in Libya. Fenech was an associate of Erik Prince, founder of the disgraced private military company formerly known as Blackwater.

The scars from the burned plane were still visible on the road beside the airport when we came home, but the story vanished, as so many others had, and nothing was mentioned about it again.

About a week after the plane crash, I was sitting at my desk with the window open when my curtains suddenly pushed inward, as though a big puff of air had hit them, but there was no breeze. The sound of a massive explosion followed moments later.

"Jesus fuck, that was a big one!" I said. "There are supposed to be limits to what those idiots can let off."

I went back to my work, but a column of smoke from the far side of the airport made it clear that this wasn't just the usual excesses of the interminable village feast. An entire stockpile of petards had exploded, flattening a barn, destroying several cars belonging to "fireworks enthusiasts," and shattering windows over a wide radius.

The explosives were being stored illegally in a farmer's field near the village of Gudja, right next to the airport runway, but no one bothered to investigate who they belonged to or why they went off. Such issues were overshadowed by the miraculous survival of a goat pulled from the rubble of the collapsed barn the next day. The farmer, a Mr. Catania, told the *Times of Malta* that he had decided to rename this goat Lucky. "You'd have to be pretty lucky to survive something like that," he said. He looked at the smoldering ruins where a building used to be and pointed at a severed head. "That sheep was less fortunate."

There were other explosions that year too. Car bombs were on the increase again—three already by October 2016, and six the year before. They happened in broad daylight, in busy commuter traffic. Of the thirteen Mafia-style killings that had taken place since we'd moved to Malta, not a single car bombing or shooting had been solved. The village squares crackled with rumors about links to drug smuggling and human trafficking, or fuel smuggling from Libya, but the increase in violent executions also coincided with the deepening web of government corruption that had swept the island since the election of Joseph Muscat.

It was easy to point the finger at mysterious foreign assassins, but no one pointed out the obvious fact that, with so many amateur fireworks factories on the island, untraced explosives were very easy to obtain.

# THE YEAR OF THE
# OLIGARCHS

Two years after being elected prime minister, Joseph Muscat made
a secret trip to Azerbaijan in December 2014 with Keith Schembri,
Konrad Mizzi, and Muscat's head of communications, Kurt Farrugia.
The prime minister's ties to the country dated back to 2007, when he
was a member of the European Parliament for Malta and a member
of the European Union–Azerbaijan parliamentary committee. The
trip was unannounced and unaccompanied by press, ambassadors,
and civil servants. Daphne only found out about it when a photo was
published in the Azeri news. A second trip took place four months
later. They agreed to bring along a few journalists this time because
of the previous outcry, but unfortunately members of the press were
on a separate flight, and a miscommunication about the arrange-
ments meant they were "delayed" in Paris and didn't arrive until the
government delegation was already home. No one knows what was
discussed.

At this point in the story, conflicts of interest begin to resemble
corporate inbreeding. Brian Tonna's accounting firm NexiaBT—the
firm that opened secret Panama companies for Mizzi and Schembri—had been hired to advise the government on a new power station project that was Labour's main electoral promise. They chose the

government's preferred solution: to convert the old Delimara power station from bunker oil to liquefied petroleum gas (LPG), using a tanker ship tethered to the plant as storage. And they were involved in selecting Electrogas as the winning bidder.

Electrogas was jointly owned by Maltese conglomerate GEM Holdings, German giant Siemens, and Socar, Azerbaijan's state energy company, who each held 33 percent of the shares. The accounting firm should never have been involved in the bidding process. They were the official auditor of GEM Holdings, the Maltese consortium fronted by business tycoon Yorgen Fenech, who was also one of Electrogas's three directors. And Tonna was the auditor for Keith Schembri's Kasco Group.

The Electrogas deal included an eighteen-year purchase agreement with Socar for LPG to run the power station, but Azerbaijan produces oil, not LPG. Socar was buying gas from Shell and reselling it to Malta for a fixed price several times higher than market rates. The timing of Muscat's visit to Baku had begun raising all sorts of questions.

Gas deals with Azerbaijan weren't the only source of income the Inner Circle would draw on. Maltese citizenship was also for sale, courtesy of the company Henley & Partners, and this may have helped the Muscat mob take power. Henley was run by Swiss lawyer Christian Kaelin, known in some circles as "the Passport King." The firm allegedly worked hand in hand with SCL Elections, parent company of Cambridge Analytica, the consultancy firm that made headlines around the world when they were hauled in front of a UK House of Commons committee investigating the misuse of private social media data. SCL was in the business of winning elections. According to whistleblower testimony in the Commons, their tactics included bribery, honey pots, prostitutes, and fake stings. SCL went in and won elections, and then Henley & Partners allegedly came in to sell that country's passports.

Kaelin had asked SCL to introduce him to Joseph Muscat in June 2011, when Muscat was still leader of the opposition. He also pitched his passport scheme to the governing Nationalist party, but they were not interested. The slick, heavily bankrolled campaign Labour ran two years later suggests that SCL may have thrown its weight behind Muscat.

The prime minister told *Bloomberg Business Week* in late 2013— just months after his election to power—that he was "interested in bringing in all those reputable people, who are willing to take up residence in Malta." He clarified that "due diligence and choosing the right type of person will be paramount." Daphne Caruana Galizia was the first to realize that details of the scheme had been strategically hidden in the *Government Gazette*. She said it revealed that Muscat's government was planning to sell passports for cash. It wouldn't take long for her claim to prove true.

Muscat went to Brussels with Kaelin in January 2014 to tell a shocked European Commission that Malta would start selling Maltese (European Union) citizenship for a base "investment" of €650,000, plus €25,000 each for dependents, and €150,000 in government stock redeemable after five years. There was little the European Union could do to stop him. Granting citizenship was the prerogative of individual member states. No one had foreseen the possibility that a member state would stoop so low, or be so opportunistic, as to sell Schengen Area passports out the back door, granting access to other people's countries whether those countries approved it or not.

The commission insisted on including the obligatory purchase or rental of property in Malta for a five-year residency period to ensure some real tie to the country, but there was no shortage of people willing to rent empty basement flats in obscure villages to a Russian oligarch or a rich Middle Easterner they would never see. Malta was also required to publish the names of individuals who had acquired citizenship by investment. They complied but printed them alongside those of naturalized citizens, with no way to differentiate between the two. The list was also alphabetized by first name to make it even more difficult for journalists to link members of the same family who purchased citizenship en masse.

It would quickly become the most valuable passport in the Henley & Partners portfolio, a clear cut above Saint Kitts and Nevis or European fringe state Moldova. It was a lucrative deal for the tiny island nation too, with reported revenues of over €1 billion in the first eighteen months. By 2016 the Individual Investor Program accounted for 2.8 percent of the Maltese economy.

But as Daphne repeatedly warned, all was never quite as it appeared. The 2021 Passport Papers leak would eventually reveal that Henley & Partners sent a circular to staff notifying them of the concession contract with the Maltese government and advising them they could start pitching this new European Union passport to clients, begin the application process, and take money before the project was even launched. The residency requirement would prove just as flexible. The checklist used to determine an applicant's "genuine link" to Malta included items like joining a club or signing up for a mobile or internet plan. Applicants could earn 50 points by donating €10,000 to a charity of their choice—including the charity fronted by the prime minister's wife—and 100 points for buying a property. This accounted for the largest portion of the 220 points required for a pass, and contrary to what Malta had told the European Union, applicants didn't even have to live there.

In the first years of the program, 1,300 of the 2,325 applications submitted came from Saudi Arabia, China, and Russia, of which the first two prohibit dual citizenship. But Maltese officials were always happy to help. Clients were advised to discuss issues in "face-to-face" meetings with the CEO of the Malta Individual Investor Program at the time, Jonathan Cardona.

What little domestic backlash to the program had existed—"It's degrading to peddle the citizenship our ancestors fought for"—dissolved in an instant when the government opened up the ability for any law firm, consultant, or estate agent to make a commission for "introducing" applicants and renting or selling a property to them. Everyone was happy, and everyone took a cut—including (allegedly) the prime minister's chief of staff. An FIAU investigation revealed that in 2016 alone, three Russians transferred a total of €167,000 through Pilatus Bank, €100,000 of which went to Keith Schembri by way of Brian Tonna, whose NexiaBT was also an agent for passport applications.

The rot went deeper than a third-degree burn. They were building an entire economy on vice: online gaming, medical cannabis, prostitution, shady financial services, and an enormous appetite for drugs. Huge profits were being made out of construction, with new buildings being thrown up everywhere; the quality was so poor it looked like they were erecting ruins.

By 2017 tiny Malta had the fourth-highest number of homicides per capita in the European Union, the worst air quality, and the world's fourth highest rate of asthma.

By 2020 two-thirds of the country's traffic police—including a superintendent—would be arrested in connection with a scam that saw them billing hundreds of hours of overtime for work they never performed. They were also accused of stealing fuel from the police garage for personal use or for sale and running a protection racket, taking money from construction companies and transport firms to look the other way on enforcement. Enraged at being caught, disgraced cops hunted down the whistleblower while the Malta police tried to convince what was left of the honest citizenry that it was investigating itself. Even for the police, *omertà* was more important than upholding the law they'd taken an oath to protect. It wasn't the person who committed the crime but the person who snitched who was guilty.

A new vindictiveness had also come to the surface, most evident in the social media hate groups that targeted Daphne and other critics of the regime, depicting non–Labour Party politicians as satanic demons and their supporters as traitors, and posting the personal details of anticorruption activists with calls for them to be physically attacked, sexually assaulted, and stalked.

As the art historian Camille Paglia wrote, "Society is not the criminal but the force which keeps crime in check. When social controls weaken, man's innate cruelty bursts forth." But no government can seize power and operate a kleptocracy without widespread support. How many circles rippled out from those main players, perhaps with diminishing knowledge of the actual crimes but equally driven by easy gain, content to keep their mouths shut as long as they got a few crumbs from the table? How many bankers, accounting firms, and lawyers sniffed the scent of rot but were gorging too much from the trough to sound the alarm?

The masses of people on the take, for whom Muscat was simply *il-King*, the people who placed his photo in their homes and lit candles before it, benefited from the public purse in the usual ways: nonjobs, permits, crumbs from the table. But every shady, undeserved perk made the job holder an accomplice to the crimes of the government. Their livelihood—their material existence—was now dependent on the political interest of the Muscat regime, and they had no choice but to defend it. Anything that threatened to bring an end to his reign was a direct threat to whatever benefit they were receiving and a personal affront, something to be met with rage. The true inner circle, those at the heart of this takeover, this bleeding of the country for personal gain, probably amounted to no more than half a dozen men. But those who defended them and kept them in power were responsible too.

My friend Victor summed it up. "Malta has always been the whore of the Mediterranean," he said, "selling its soul for money no matter where it comes from. We don't mind corruption—when it's on our side." This was just the modern expression of the piracy the island had always been known for. In Malta, corruption had always been seen as an opportunity rather than a badge of shame.

After months of being bombarded by such scandals, it had all begun to seem very dull and very normal. But Malta also began to feel like a place where anything could be done to you without anyone ever hearing about it. Especially if you were an outsider.

John Paul Cauchi wrote in the *Times* that "it is clear that in Malta we don't elect prime ministers. We elect god-kings. Cult worship ensues."

The governing party wielded enormous power, embodied in the office of the prime minister. Every appointee from every institution that mattered answered directly to him and was indebted to him for their job. Muscat used this—systematically, deliberately—to exploit each of the country's institutional weaknesses. In hindsight it was easy to see how he'd done it.

The country went through five police commissioners in four years, all appointed directly by the prime minister. John Rizzo, a man known for being tough on corruption, and who had arrested and prosecuted Malta's chief justice for soliciting bribes, was dismissed and replaced one month after Labour took power. He would be followed in quick succession by Peter Paul Zammit (an ineffective puppet), Ray Zammit (forced to resign in the wake of scandals involving his two sons,

both corrupt cops), Michael Cassar (who quit rather than prosecute
Mizzi and Schembri), and finally Lawrence Cutajar, who had praised
the prime minister's brass balls on Facebook.

The rank and file were co-opted next. Muscat's home affairs
minister reinstated some seventy-six police officers, ages fifty-five to
eighty, and put them on the payroll in 2014. Many were dragged out
of retirement and given backdated promotions, regardless of their
physical condition, obesity, or total decrepitude. Several had criminal
records, including one who was previously dismissed from the force
for hitting a woman while on duty. All were connected to the Labour
Party.

The military was taken care of too. In late 2013 Maj. Jeffrey Curmi,
a close family friend of the Muscats, was promoted three times in
three months, rocketing from major to brigadier general before being
appointed commander of the Armed Forces of Malta. The same
process was followed with the head of every regulatory body, all of
whom were appointed by the prime minister, either directly or on his
"recommendation."

The result was a total impunity that would gradually trickle down
to all levels of Maltese society. The police did little investigating, even
when reports landed in their laps, and Attorney General Peter Grech
declined to prosecute. When it came to taking action against Muscat's inner circle, they could be relied on to do nothing at all.

The attorney general's role came with its own set of structural
problems, having been constitutionally charged with the dual role of
both public prosecutor and adviser to the government. It must have
been exhausting for him to handle courtroom cases of political corruption, shuttling back and forth from one side of the room to the
other as he played both offense and defense, tasked with defending
the government's interests while protecting Joseph Muscat's.

Those few enforcement bodies that fought to maintain a semblance of impartiality, like the FIAU, were left deliberately understaffed, starved of resources at a time when they should have been investigating cases of financial corruption that had long been public knowledge. The parliamentary ombudsman and the auditor general were undermined through both lack of resources and a failure to act on their findings. And the Permanent Commission Against Corruption hadn't produced any results in its thirty-year existence.

The entire structure was stacked in Muscat's favor, but he needed to keep a tight rein on the system to avoid being punished after he left office. He appointed loyal individuals to key roles and gave backbench MPs well-paid positions as persons of trust or advisers to public bodies, which made them beholden to the executive for their very livelihood. Other individuals were deliberately compromised so that their hands would be dirty, too. As the novelist Philip Roth said, "It's what the mafia does. You give someone something they can't talk about, and you've got them."

Muscat's power grew along with his sense that he could do no wrong in the eyes of his party-blind worshippers. The Panama Papers revelations threw a wrench in their plans but didn't derail them. Mizzi was removed as Labour Party deputy leader and demoted from energy minister, but he still signed the corrupt Electrogas deal and another lucrative public-private partnership that saw the government hand over three public hospitals to a mysterious consortium run by an Indian Canadian fraudster with no prior health-care experience. The government refused to table these deals in parliament, citing "commercial sensitivity." Freedom of Information requests were also denied; even when the government lost a case on appeal, they still refused to comply. No one could force them to obey a court order: the police had been compromised long ago. By this point it no longer seemed abnormal to have the governing party refusing to share massive commercial contracts with the rest of parliament, despite having signed these agreements in their name.

After ceremonially demoting Mizzi, Muscat absorbed more and more portfolios, assimilating the departments of disgraced cabinet members into the Office of the Prime Minister. By the end of 2019 he had assumed responsibility for financial services, online gaming, cryptocurrency, tourism, private-public partnerships, Malta Enterprise (including cannabis), and citizenship and visas—all sectors that combined massive revenues with a high risk of money laundering and corruption.

But not everyone jumped aboard the Muscat gravy train. A handful of journalists remained defiant, and though justice could be stalled through endless delaying tactics and through secretive magisterial inquiries, the courts remained an obstacle and a threat.

The judiciary would be the last to fall. After being tasked by an increasingly alarmed Council of Europe to conduct a review into Malta's institutions, the Venice Commission stated in very clear terms that the prime minister should not have the power to appoint judges. Muscat agreed with their recommendations—and then rushed through three judicial appointments before the system could be reformed.

Years later, after it had all become a fait accompli, former European Court of Human Rights judge Giovanni Bonello would say, "The executive power of the state, which means the prime minister and the cabinet, have virtually taken over all the other institutions which were meant to control the executive. The attorney general, the commissioner of police, parts of the judiciary are more than suspect. They give the impression they are in the pocket of the persons they are supposed to keep in check." When asked how it had gone so wrong, Bonello said, "A system is as good as the people who put it in practice. It matters in any circumstance, but particularly so when one of the chief suspects of ill-doing is the government itself, is the executive itself. It is under a suspicious pall of being in league with major criminals."

After a year of heated speculation, Daphne published a story on April 19, 2017, claiming that she knew who owned Egrant, the mysterious third Panama company opened at the same time as those belonging to Konrad Mizzi and Keith Schembri. She included a photo of the prime minister's wife sitting next to Leyla Aliyeva, daughter of Azerbaijan's ruling strongman, and wrote that Aliyeva "transferred very large sums of money, described as 'loan payments,' to Hearnville Inc., Tillgate Inc. and Egrant Inc. last year." She would reveal the rest the next day.

The entire country held its breath, hitting "refresh" until the update appeared. Everyone expected her to name the prime minister, but Daphne claimed that the ultimate beneficial owner of the third company mentioned in the Panama Papers—the one too sensitive to name by email—was Joseph Muscat's wife. She backed her story with a copy of the corporate registry, obtained from a whistleblower within Pilatus Bank. The original was held in a safe in the bank's kitchen, she said, where it was shielded from CCTV by European Union data protection laws that forbid surveillance in employee break rooms. Her source said the safe also contained documents related to Russian clients, and to Maltese politically exposed persons (PEPs) including Keith Schembri, whose account allegedly showed highly suspicious transactions involving people in Azerbaijan.

One of Muscat's first acts after coming to power had been to order a revision of the ministerial code of ethics. Cabinet members no longer had to include assets owned by their spouses or underage children in their annual declarations. If Michelle Muscat really did own Egrant, as Daphne claimed, it was safely distanced from the prime minister.

Joseph Muscat sprang into action minutes later with an evening press conference filled with angry denials, calling it "the biggest political lie ever told in this country." I would have expected him to express outrage at the immorality of the act he was being accused of, but instead he was curiously careful with his words. "We never signed any type of document which transfers shares of a company," he said. "I have never signed, never been offered to sign…"

When asked whether he would call for an investigation, the prime minister declined. He would let the country's institutions do their job. Meanwhile, his pet police commissioner nibbled rabbit in a distant corner of the island with his buddies and refused to comment.

That same night, Ali Sadr Hasheminejad was caught on camera by Net News slipping out the back door of Pilatus Bank with risk manager Antoniella Gauchi and beetling down the street with two heavy bags. The reporter gasped a steady stream of questions as he struggled to keep up: "Do you work for Pilatus Bank? Why were you there so late at night?" Ali Sadr stared straight ahead, dodging around corners with grim determination, crossing and recrossing the same empty street. His face only broke into a smirk when he dumped the bags into the trunk of a car. As he got in the passenger seat, he turned to his pursuer and said, "I have no idea what you're talking about, and you'd better learn some English to ask some questions." The reporter didn't know that the young man with the greased-back hair who'd just slipped away was the bank's owner.

Then Flight Radar showed a chartered jet leaving Malta for Baku, Azerbaijan, at 4 a.m. The plane went from there to Dubai, where Egrant was alleged to have another account. One week later, Vista-Jet—the company that carried out this empty "ferry flight"—was given €1 million in funding from Malta's tourism budget on the direct order of the Office of the Prime Minister.

Once the goose had flown, Muscat confidently ordered a raid on the bank and a magisterial inquiry into the Egrant allegations. This sudden contradiction of his televised conference, held just hours before, was announced in a Department of Information press release issued in the middle of the night. Meanwhile, the Maltese were left scratching their heads, saying, "Well, we really need some proof…"

Suitcases in the night. It all read like a bad movie. When the crisis struck, Malta was holding the rotating presidency of the European Union, and for once Europe was paying attention to this strange little island on its southernmost fringe. But Joseph Muscat was like a stubborn turd in a toilet bowl. No matter how many times he was flushed, he kept popping back up.

An army of organized Labour trolls went on the attack, targeting Daphne as a witch, liar, and traitor to Malta. When her face appeared on a Labour Party billboard, Muscat said, "If the opposition leader wants to stop his country's name from being tarnished, all he needs to do is go to Bidnija [Daphne's residence]…. People among us are attacking the country."

As the scandals multiplied and whistleblowers revealed documented evidence of criminal rot, kickbacks, and money laundering through a web of offshore corporations and accounts, the prime minister called a snap election one year ahead of schedule to divert attention from the growing number of magisterial inquiries into the shady dealings of his closest associates.

Muscat's expressions had always reminded me of an angry toddler or someone who was clearly bullied in school. But as he fought for his very survival, his accent changed from fake and controlled to a village dialect that spiraled into hysterics, and his eyes took on a cold, hard glare anytime he was asked about Egrant. It was only then that I realized this man could be dangerous. But the prime minister also looked increasingly haggard, with a pallor of sleeplessness and a visible loss of weight. Civil society anticorruption rallies were attracting

larger and larger numbers of followers, and the opposition Nationalist Party leader, Simon Busuttil, was riding an increasingly angry wave
of support.

The Labour Party dished out nonjobs and government contracts
by direct order in the frantic lead-up to the election: more than 1,000
secure public-sector jobs were given to supporters, including 220 in
the electoral district being contested by Panama Papers minister Konrad Mizzi. More than one-third of the army received promotions, and
police officers who had retired or been dismissed for having criminal
records were reinstated. Some 588 building illegalities were regularized by the Planning Authority, 405 of them in the campaign's final
two weeks. Members of parliament handed out "hampers" of cheap
food: bottles of wine labeled with the face of "Il-Ministru Konrad
Mizzi"; bags of bread with printed inserts for Silvio Schembri; a sack
of oranges with the face and contact details of Chris Fearne. Employees in the offices of cabinet ministers called random constituents
with the same scripted approach: "Hello, madam, good afternoon.
I'm calling from Owen Bonnici's ministry to see whether you need
anything."

It didn't matter if these frantic promises were completely unwork-
able or legal. All that mattered to each voter was what was promised to
them. When asked by a visiting journalist how he felt about the current
situation, a taxi driver was quoted as saying, "They can take whatever
they want because they haven't taken it from me and I don't care because I have money in my pocket." If he was in a position of power, he'd
do it too, so he couldn't understand why anyone would not.

Knowing full well what was at stake, the Maltese people didn't just
choose to look the other way with corruption; they voted in favor of
it. Joseph Muscat was reelected with a larger majority. In the inevitable aftermath of gloating car parades, Labour Party supporters were
filmed celebrating in front of Pilatus Bank.

Daphne's blog went silent for days after the results came in. The entire country had turned against her: Labour supporters for having the nerve to "attack" their king with her Egrant accusation, and Nationalist supporters who blamed an independent journalist for their party's loss. I emailed to see if she was okay. "Not really," she said, writing back within hours. "It was bad enough dealing with the fact that I live in a country with a corrupt government and decimated institutions. Now I have to face the fact that the population itself is corrupt and amoral."

Despite this depressing outcome, she wasn't surprised that Muscat had won. In her first article after the election, she wrote:

> The problem that has to be addressed is the widespread and ever-increasing amorality among a sizable percentage of the Maltese population. It spans the entire socio-economic spectrum and has nothing at all to do with social class, privilege or the lack of it. Thirty, forty years ago, this amorality could have been excused on the grounds of illiteracy and ignorance, of Malta's isolation from the world in a tightly controlled and insular environment. Now, there is no such excuse and we have to face the brutal fact of what we are, and examine how it has come about and whether there are any solutions. I happen to think, right now, that there are probably none, because amoral familism, the root cause of it, is the result of centuries of social programming.

It was only weeks later that she realized the election dates didn't add up. Everyone assumed that Muscat had called the election over Egrant, but Daphne's revelation wasn't published until April 19. The Labour Party had already chosen its slogan by mid-March and purchased domain names by the beginning of April. Henley & Partners CEO Christian Kaelin had started harassing her to take down stories about him in March "because an election is coming."

Muscat had a year left in his term and a 36,000-vote majority. He couldn't be defeated in parliament, and he wouldn't be properly investigated thanks to his control of the country's institutions. So why now?

Daphne believed something bigger was coming. "Whatever it is, it's bad enough to have driven Muscat to take drastic action just two months into Malta's much-vaunted presidency of the EU Council," she wrote. "We need to know what this thing is that they fear so much that they want it to happen after they are reelected to another term in government, and not before."

Looking back, I think she foretold her own death.

# FOUR

# POINT OF NO RETURN

# AMORAL

# FAMILISM

In 2019 the Italian political scientist Luca Ranieri attempted to explain the structural causes of Malta's rampant corruption in a study published in the *European Review of Organized Crime*. One of his takeaways was that corruption was endemic to Malta in part because of geography. As a small island state with few natural resources, located at a crossroads in the middle of the Mediterranean, tapping into the transnational economic flows passing back and forth across that sea had always been vital to the country's survival. But geography and resource scarcity didn't determine Malta's penchant for shady dealing. The factors were also deeply cultural.

Raineri built a convincing case that Malta is an attractive haven for organized crime for four main reasons. It acted as a gateway into the European Union for illicit economic flows that would normally be blocked from the European market. Maltese middlemen received and transshipped fuel smuggled from war-torn Libya, for example, and Italian mafia cash was laundered through Maltese online gambling companies, which Ranieri referred to as "an ATM with continual cash flow." The country's citizenship-by-investment scheme also acted as a back door into other member states for dubious characters who would otherwise raise red flags.

That endless international supply of corruption was welcomed by "political entrepreneurs" who were eager to expand their clientele. These were men with a foothold in both politics and business, like the prime minister's chief of staff, Keith Schembri; cabinet minister, Konrad Mizzi; and the fuel smuggler Darren Debono, all named in Ranieri's report. Malta offered opaque structures where such people could conceal their beneficial ownership behind trusts and companies fronted by a local lawyer, often someone politically connected. Local strongmen made sure these dubious transactions were protected from police interference.

According to Ranieri, Malta wasn't a mafia state or a failed state. On the contrary, it was a success story where "economic and political elites seem to look at the proliferation of victimless forms of crime such as money laundering and fuel smuggling less as a threat than as an opportunity." It was "a corrupting island in a corrupting sea."

Daphne Caruana Galizia believed that the substratum of Maltese corruption was amoral familism, a predatory family-centric ethos first theorized by the American political scientist Edward Banfield in *The Moral Basis of a Backward Society*, his study of a rural village in Southern Italy. "Nobody can seek to understand Maltese politics or Maltese society without first understanding amoral familism," she wrote on her blog. It "shapes and drives both—and it has ruined both."

Banfield may have introduced the concept of amoral familism to the world, but it was applied to Malta by anthropologist Jeremy Boissevain, whose ideas I first encountered in *Saints and Fireworks*, still the seminal work of Maltese ethnography. The year was 1961, and Boissevain was living in the southern village of Kirkop, where he was writing a thesis on the cult of the saints. He would go on to write about amoral familism in *Factions, Friends, and Feasts*, where he described it as "part of the fabric of daily life" that "exists in a particularly concentrated form in Malta because of the importance of the family and the close-knit, small-scale, face-to-face character of the crowded islands and the legacy of alien domination." Amoral familism is an ultimately self-destructive form of extreme self-interest where any action undertaken to benefit one's family or oneself is justifiable and everyone expects everyone else to do whatever benefits their family or themselves, regardless of whether it is legal or ethical.

After studying this concept, all those inexplicable aspects of Maltese life I'd encountered lined up as though the wheels of a cipher had locked into place. I saw amoral familism in the subtle ways people tried to fuck others over—the surface appearance of friendliness that concealed petty cunning. I saw it in the way squatters built shanties on stolen bits of coastline at Armier Bay: "Why shouldn't I have a beach house if I want one?" I saw it in the dumping of rubbish in the countryside: "It's not my home—who cares?" I saw it in the out-of-control illegal building: "I want a new addition / an extra story / a new building on protected land.... I'll just build it anyway and bribe a politician to legalize it later." And I saw it in the way landlords and property agents would tell me anything to get me to agree to something while never having any intention of sticking to their word; they'd go behind my back at the first opportunity to make a deal with someone else if they thought it was to their advantage.

Maltese life was a world of nested hierarchies, of binary oppositions that diminished in scale like a stack of Russian dolls. There was the island versus the outside world; Malta versus the European Union; Nationalist versus Labour; *tal-pepe* versus *hamalli;* the progressive north versus the backward south; and my village versus your village, especially the village next door. Within that village, my band club versus your band club; my saint versus your saint; and my festa versus your festa. Then we strike true bedrock, the foundation stone of Maltese culture, my family versus everyone else.

As Daphne wrote, amoral familism was the engine that drove

Malta's astonishingly high levels of voter turnout: "Amoral familism is the reason people in Malta use their vote as currency and do not think in terms of the common good or choosing the right government, but in terms of spiting/rewarding, getting/preventing others from getting. It is also the reason why even monied and supposedly educated individuals are not embarrassed—rather, they are proud because they think it is a heroic act and that it is perfectly normal and civilized—to talk openly about not voting for this or that party, or not voting at all, on the basis of personal matters and what they wish to obtain personally (or prevent others from obtaining)."

Seen through the lens of amoral familism, each family was pitted against every other family in a zero-sum competition for resources, where people felt entitled to take as much as they could for themselves because everyone else was doing it too. To take an extreme example, let's say a neighbor had a handicapped child, and they were given financial benefits. That would have nothing to do with me, but as an amoral familist, I should see their "gain" as my loss. The amoral familist would consider himself worse off if his neighbor's position changed for the better, and he might even vote against measures that help the community without helping him.

Anyone who stood outside the small circle of the family was a potential competitor and a potential enemy. You had to be especially wary if you were doing well. Others would inevitably envy and fear the success of your family, and you had to be ready to do them an injury so they'd have less power to injure you. In such situations the Maltese gossip network acted as a system of social control. If someone was becoming too successful, everyone around them tried to pull that person down. But if that person succeeded regardless and became too big to undermine, their position shifted and they were regarded as a source of patronage and influence. The backstabbing gossips became fawning bootlickers instead.

Some scholars have taken exception to Banfield's original conception of amoral familism in his work on Italy—though not, as
far as I'm aware, with Boissevain's application to Malta—and that's
understandable because it is a rather ugly theory. Amoral familism
shouldn't be taken as a blanket condemnation of Maltese society
or of all Maltese people. Instead, it should be regarded as a survival
strategy that formed deep roots in the culture, in part because it was
successful. I can understand how such a worldview might have developed. On an island that had always lacked natural resources, and that
was far too overpopulated to support its own people, "wealth" came
from outside. It was finite and was either distributed like a boon from
colonial overlords or grasped frantically before someone else took it
first. Under such conditions, it becomes easy to justify stealing from
those in charge, or taking a little more for oneself and one's family, or
skimming off public funds. Stealing from colonial rulers or indulging
in a little piracy was tolerated too, and some outside power always
reined it in when it went too far.

Amoral familism made life miserable for many, but it worked in
a closed island setting composed of isolated villages, each playing by
those same grasping rules in what was often a desperate struggle to
survive.

Centuries of powerlessness formed a culture that was perfectly
adapted to parasite off a stronger conquering power. With Malta's
accession to the European Union, the scant resources from the outside world that this barren island relied on for its survival became an
unlimited flow of funding. And when Joseph Muscat was elected and
the Labour Party returned to power, amoral familism cascaded out
of control.

A dweller in a Maltese village lives under conditions of near-panoptical
surveillance. Every purchase is remembered by a shopkeeper who also

knows your parents, your wife, and your ancestors. You can't walk to the post office without your movements being tracked and analyzed, not just by old men loafing on the steps of the church but by all those eyes peering out of windows from behind lace curtains. That's how I thought of the undistinguished sprawl of row houses at the edge of every village: a conspiracy of houses, and above them on a wire, a murder of crows.

I found the speed of the local bush telegraph comical, but this gossip network had a dark side too. Watchfulness was a form of social control. Conformity was enforced by neighbors, and as in any authoritarian situation they got ahead by snitching. Telling the teacher. Ratting out their neighbor to the priest or the Inquisition. Smacking down originality by making those who dared to be different the subject of malicious slander.

I met a Canadian lady who lived in another village in the south with her Maltese husband. "Once you're married," she told me, "you must always and only go out with your husband or with your children. Our house is off a narrow alley, with several houses at the other end. Every time I leave home alone, I see all the neighbors looking at me and judging me. As though having a life or interests beyond my family means I must be up to something." They suspected others of the evil within their own hearts. The caged birds resented the freedom of the one who flies and sings.

The ethnographical literature on Malta confirms this. Anthropologist Jon Mitchell spent time with a Valletta family when he was doing research for his book *Ambivalent Europeans*. "I was constantly being told by well-meaning acquaintances that under no circumstances should I let them know about my private affairs," he wrote. "To do so would be dangerous, even with particularly close friends."

Friendships in Malta had always struck me as surface friendly, composed of joking or superficial conversations without any real depth. Perhaps it was because everyone was so guarded.

"Problems of a personal nature should be discussed with either family members or a priest," Mitchell continued. "Under no circumstances should they be made public amongst a group of male friends. To do so would be to invite its abuse in local gossip." An informant summed it up best when he told Mitchell, "Not everyone who strokes you, loves you. Be careful." Meaning, "Although people might seem to be generous or friendly, trusting them because of this is a mistake."

The islanders had developed an ability to switch back and forth between different versions of their lives and to believe both simultaneously. Corruption was always something done by someone else: the other political party, the neighbor whose possessions they envied, or the big property developer. And when they themselves evaded taxes, broke laws with impunity, or benefited from shady deals, that was different: "*U ejja!* It's always been like this. Everybody does it! Don't wurr-ry!"

Laws were meant to be got around rather than obeyed. If they got caught and suffered punishment, they didn't feel guilty. They were a victim, just unlucky.

I thought it was childish for grown adults to say things like, "Well, Charlie did it too and he got away with it, so why are you picking on me?" But though it's a logical fallacy, in the Maltese setting, whataboutism was an admissible argument. That person was saying, "You acted to benefit your own political party, and to hell with everyone else, so what's wrong with what we did?" It conformed to the amoral familism worldview rather than moral right or wrong. A political party mirrored a family, because it reflected that person's identity. A Maltese person was either Labour or Nationalist. Red or Blue. That person would do whatever benefited the Labour or Nationalist party while expecting everyone in the other party to be doing the same.

A regular newspaper commentator provided the best explanation for how the gears of Maltese society are oiled. "One, has this person done anything wrong to me personally or my family?" he wrote. "And Two, has this person talked to me amiably? If the answer to One is 'no' and Two is 'yes,' I guess they're *orrajt*. Brownie points are given for positive references from people close to me—never mind if their analysis is even worse than mine—and church attendance of the person in question. Golden points are awarded if they're willing to help me out in something fishy. Then mix in some vague fear of revenge or negative repercussions to my descendants somewhere down the line in the next 100 years, should I point out that there's something wrong with this person. The usual excuse is that 'everyone' knows already, so why should I be the one to bell the cat?"

This fear of retribution was pervasive. According to Boissevain, "Most Maltese have personally experienced and/or know of persons who have been punished for criticizing their neighbors, superiors, government policy, or influential persons, or for reporting some illegal activity."

Front doors and vehicles were set on fire in the night. Permits, scholarships, and contracts were refused. Expected promotions were suddenly called off. Critical news media, activists, and NGOs were subject to punitive libel suits and withheld advertising. And, in our case, the flower pots outside our front door in Zejtun were smashed one after the other.

But fear of retribution went deeper than just a reluctance to speak up. Centuries of amoral familism had bred a form of cowardice where hiding was considered an intelligent survival skill.

"We'd like change to happen," Dr. Dalli told me, "but we're unwilling to expose ourselves to retaliation. You hear people complaining of some illegality but refusing to report it officially because they don't want to have to testify in court 'so as not to make enemies.' Seeing others punished merely encourages a nation of people who are already incredibly spineless to find justification for their paltry choices... reassurance that they're right to cower beneath the parapet, hoping the government will be so busy eating others alive that it won't notice them." He shrugged. "There are a thousand dogs for every bone on this benighted island, and we've been trained from birth to be cowardly and character-free so as to survive and make money."

Such behavior was reinforced by an entire series of proverbs in praise of spinelessness. *Omm il-gifa qatt ma gheliet* tells us that the parents of cowards never have to worry, or to endure grief. And *Tbus l-id li tixtieqha maqtugha* says that it is necessary to grovel and scrape before a bully.

Shutting one's mouth—the all-pervasive *omertà*—had its own related set of proverbs, such as *Min jgħid wisq ftit fih risq*, meaning people who speak a lot are bad news, and *Aħjar kelma nieqsa minn kelma zejda*, one word less is better than an extra word. This is regarded as wise advice because in Malta, *L-ajru għandu għajnu, u l-ħajt għandu widintu*, the air has eyes and the walls have ears. One should police their thoughts and speech even when chatting with friends or family. Taking a stand or speaking up is foolish, because a lone voice never got anywhere.

The general mentality was to survive rather than thrive. *Aħjar hekk inkella agħar* reminds us that it can always be worse. Such proverbs instilled a sense of resignation, an ingrained fatalism that says if you just wait long enough, one set of rulers will be replaced by another.

That anxiousness to please, the desperation to stay neutral, made sense to me when seen through the lens of amoral familism. In some ways it was an island mentality, the necessity of keeping the peace among people confined to a small place: *Ma niksirha ma' ħadd,* meaning I don't burn bridges with anyone. But it went deeper than social harmony. Speaking up or taking a stand doesn't serve your short-term interest or the short-term interest of the immediate family. It's better to wait for someone else to take the risk. By hiding, you'll still benefit from the outcome without doing any of the work.

People did eventually jump sides, but they only rushed to stick the knife in Caesar's back once the outcome had already been decided. They sat on the fence and waited to see which way the wind would blow and then committed to the winning side because they didn't want to miss the rewards. But dependency also built resentment. Constant complaining released the pressure just enough to prevent a meltdown, and a culture of mutual griping reinforced that, yes, we are victims, and we're all just as fucked by forces beyond our control.

# POINT OF NO RETURN

In the last email I had from her, in mid-June 2017, Daphne wrote: "Life here in Malta is set to regress to what I knew growing up in the 1970s and 1980s—minus the human rights violations and the open physical violence, one hopes."

She had seen it all coming so clearly, but she was helpless to affect the outcome. A vacuum formed around her as she was systematically dehumanized in social media hate groups, targeted through the courts with malicious libel suits, and verbally attacked by politicians. She was the voice of so many people, but they let her stand alone because they feared becoming the target of that same relentless retaliation. And when she'd been sufficiently isolated, she could be killed.

She died on a Monday afternoon in October 2017, minutes after she had left her home to run an errand. The bomb that had been placed beneath the driver's seat of her car was detonated as she drove down the slope of a rural valley past dry stone walls and carefully cultivated farms. I could picture that road so clearly. I'd driven it several times to visit an expat friend who must have been her neighbor, ten minutes away from my old Mosta flat.

Contrary to initial reports, there were two explosions, not one. The first tore her leg off, but she'd only just begun to scream when a larger explosion engulfed her car in a ball of fire. The burning shell continued downhill, missing the curve and rolling to a stop in a dirt-filled field, its doors twisted on their frames and the roof buckled upward from the force of the blast.

A neighbor who had been driving toward her slammed on his brakes and jumped out of his car. When he saw body parts strewn across the road, he blocked the path to stop others from driving over them.

Daphne's son Matthew was first on the scene. He ran down the hill barefoot, in a blind panic, but he must have known what had happened from the timing of the sound that shook the valley. He posted a statement on Facebook the next morning. "I looked down and there were my mother's body parts all around me," he wrote. "I am sorry for being graphic, but this is what war looks like, and you need to know. This was no ordinary murder and it was not tragic. Tragic is someone being run over by a bus. When there is blood and fire all around you, that's war. We are a people at war against the state and organized crime, which have become indistinguishable."

By the time Daphne's husband, Peter, reached the site from Valletta, the road was already filled with police cars. The family's worst fear had finally come true. Just the day before, he and Daphne had gone to lunch in Naxxar and bought plants for the garden she cultivated with such care. We know this because they were followed and photographed by Neville Gafa, an associate of the prime minister's chief of staff, who posted them online as part of the targeted campaign against her.

As he walked up to the waiting police officer, Peter looked at the smoldering wreck of his wife's car in the field and said, "Is she dead?"

Daphne died with forty-two libel suits still pending against her, including nineteen cases from businessman Silvio Debono's DB Group alone. The rest had been filed by politicians. But no politicians were questioned by police, and those who had the most to benefit from her silencing—Joseph Muscat, Konrad Mizzi, Keith Schembri, Chris Cardona, and the rest—remained in power.

None of the island's earlier car bombs had been solved, but this one was different. Acting on his own initiative, Counter Terrorism Unit head George Cremona contacted the FBI to provide Malta with assistance within an hour and a half of Daphne's murder. "I was sure that if they came to Malta they could provide services for triangulation and data mining," he said years later in testimony before a public inquiry. "I contacted counterparts in Rome." Then he informed the police commissioner, Lawrence Cutajar.

The Americans traced the mobile phones used to set off the device and reconstructed the hitmen's movements in the days, hours, and moments leading up to the explosion with help from Europol and Dutch experts.

Arrests were made at the beginning of December with a theatrical raid on a dockside potato shed in Marsa that involved helicopters, military vehicles, AFM patrol boats, masked special forces operatives, and the Malta police. The entire show was filmed and broadcast online in what felt like a Hollywood-style PR campaign. Sure enough, when it came time to announce the arrests to the media, it was the prime minister who strutted to the podium rather than his pet police commissioner.

The Marsa hangout where the raid took place was a nest of criminality frequented by people involved in everything from prostitution to more serious—and more dangerous—crimes. The ten suspects were all well known to police, but none had been written about by Daphne, and it's unlikely they'd ever read her.

Years later Deputy Prime Minister Chris Fearne was asked whether Muscat had discussed Daphne's assassination with him. Fearne said he had, right after the three hitmen were arrested. "He told me, 'We've solved it.'" But Muscat also played the martyr, adding, "This is the worst thing that could have happened to me." One wonders if he was referring to the assassination or to those responsible—who might be able to identify the masterminds—getting caught.

The three men who would eventually be charged with planting and triggering the bomb—brothers Alfred and George Degiorgio and Vince Muscat (no relation to the prime minister)—had thrown their mobile phones into the sea before the raid, and George had written his partner's phone number on his forearm. Transcripts from their initial questioning show police interrogators asking: "Who told you we were coming? How did you know we were coming? You smelled us coming?" It was clear someone inside the Malta police or the prime minister's inner circle had tipped them off.

The two brothers were bottom-feeders living conspicuous lifestyles well beyond their means. Registered as unemployed and on social benefits, they owned luxury cars and boats, vacationed in Monte Carlo, and sent their children to expensive private schools. Despite the obvious red flags, they were only charged with money laundering when stories about their lifestyle began circulating a year after they were captured.

Joseph Muscat treated the hitmen's arrest as case closed and tried to move on. A former head of Europol complained that Maltese authorities were dragging their feet when it came to investigating who commissioned the murder. Delegations from Europe sent to assess the country's failing rule of law were always told "it's in the courts" or "there's a magisterial inquiry."

But Daphne's three sons refused to let the story die. Backed by a small group of civil society protesters in Malta and press freedom groups abroad, they spent the next two years traveling from country to country, speaking on panels, addressing the Council of Europe and the United Nations, pleading for justice for their mother and their country.

Walls were painted with stenciled words—"Who Killed Daphne?"—and banners were occasionally slung across overpasses bearing her face as an accusation, but the government quickly took them down. A group of female activists calling themselves Occupy Justice held vigils on the sixteenth of each month and tended a small memorial of flowers, candles, and photos that had been placed at the base of the Great Siege Monument opposite Valletta's courthouse. These objects were shoved into garbage bags and hauled away every night by employees of the cleansing department, acting on the orders of the justice minister, Owen Bonnici. Each morning volunteers returned with fresh flowers and set them up again. The scene repeated itself every day for two years. The women were spat on by old men from a nearby café, threatened by Labour Party supporters, and sometimes physically attacked, but they would not be deterred—and neither would a handful of intrepid journalists who took up the investigations Daphne had started.

One month after Daphne's assassination, Caroline Muscat (no relation to the prime minister) started *The Shift*, an independent online investigative news portal. The former news editor of the country's oldest and most respected paper, the *Times* and the *Sunday Times of Malta*, knew that the only way to remain truly independent in a country where the government controlled the media by doling out funding and advertising was to run her entire enterprise on money donated by readers. *The Shift* soon found a powerful niche investigating major deals in Malta and helping other newsrooms trace cross-border connections to much larger stories.

A handful of breakthroughs also came from abroad. Ali Sadr Hasheminejad was arrested by the FBI in 2018 at Washington's Dulles Airport and charged in a six-count federal indictment accusing him of being involved in a scheme to evade U.S. economic sanctions against Iran. After two years of legal wrangling, he was found guilty and convicted of bank fraud for moving $115 million through an Iranian housing project in Venezuela. His conviction was later reversed in mysterious circumstances prior to sentencing. Months after his arrest, the European Central Bank revoked Pilatus's license and shut the Maltese bank down.

Other arrests were made by Italian and Spanish police in cases involving money laundering, fuel smuggling from Libya, and the sale of illicit farmed tuna—all centered on Malta. But none of these investigations were instigated by the Maltese authorities, and none were followed up on. The only thing that changed with the arrest of the Degiorgios was that all the car bombs on the island stopped.

# IT ALL
# FALLS DOWN

The threads of my own life began to converge with events in Malta when I met Caroline Muscat for dinner in Berlin's Kreuzberg district in November 2018. She entered the bar in a frazzled rush, typing on her phone, and we exchanged a few pleasantries about the city. The drinks came—white wine for her, unfiltered house beer for me—and she launched straight into her pitch.

"I know we've never spoken," she said, "but I'm a great admirer of your work. The piece you wrote for Daphne's blog remained engraved in my mind. We'd love to share your thoughts with our readers."

"I'm glad you liked that article," I said, "but I'm not a journalist. Besides, we left the island over a year ago. I'm a little out of touch."

"The things we tolerate in Malta are unacceptable," she said, ignoring my attempt at evasion. "The whole process of what's happened since Daphne's death is beyond belief. The lack of investigation, the continued hate campaign, the attack on anyone who says her name, the denial of a public inquiry. The list is too long, and I'm not sure whether people grasp this. You can bring an outside perspective to show just how abnormal things are in our country, because you lived there for so long, and you really get us."

I'd left Malta for good in January 2017, a few months before

Daphne was killed. I wanted to move on with my life in Berlin, but Caroline's story of their friendship touched me in a way that dry, fact-based news accounts of the murder hadn't. They left me angry and outraged, but Caroline reminded me of the person whose life had been cut short.

"We spoke of Europe as a godsend," she told me. "Daphne and me. We didn't trust our own politicians to get things right, so we both voted 'join' in the hope that EU membership would prevent a recurrence of past governmental abuses, and that it would exert a 'civilizing' influence. As Daphne often said, 'to show the cavemen how things are done.' And there was hope, at least for a while. But we took so much for granted. One of them was the belief that Europe would save us from our own worst impulses.

"The last thing she said to me, a few days before her assassination, was, 'I get a sense of time running out. There are so many things I wanted to do that I haven't done.' My first reaction was numbness," Caroline said. "All I could think about was that the lunch we planned for the following week would never happen."

It reminded me of the first message I had from Daphne, the day after I moved to Berlin. "All three of my sons lived there at one point," she wrote. "I visit quite often. I'm sure you will enjoy living there. I will email when I am next there." Nine months later she was dead. Missing the chance to meet her in person is one of my great regrets.

"My second reaction was to set up an independent news portal that would continue her work," Caroline said, pulling me back to the present. "The people who did this can't be allowed to get away with it." She took a sip of wine. "I'm prepared to offer a weekly space. I don't impose ideas. You can write about whatever is bubbling up inside. So... are you in?"

I said I'd take a couple days to think about it, but I already knew I couldn't walk away while the people who killed Daphne went free.

Malta is an exasperating place, but it is also strangely compelling. Working with *The Shift* brought me into contact with a different side of the island than the one I'd known during my years of residency. I met activists who fought to preserve the last remaining green spaces and brave anticorruption journalists who stuck their heads above the parapet even after Daphne was killed. They were a minority fighting against what must have felt like hopeless odds. I also received messages from readers who hated the new lows their country was sinking to under Joseph Muscat but were too frightened to speak about it in public. *The Shift* had become their voice.

Caroline did much to pull me out of the slump of my increasingly pessimistic views. She'd spent years abroad and shared my frustrations, but she also challenged my conclusions. In doing so she became a friend. My work as a columnist soon expanded to helping with editing, writing grant applications, and formulating strategies for increasing *The Shift*'s readership using the same techniques that had grown my online fitness publishing business. The months were marked by an accumulation of coffee mugs and crumb-scattered plates on the corner of my desk as we coordinated stories and tried to sort out fact from rumor.

The government was desperate to eradicate the memory of the woman who had been its harshest critic, but the truth could not be buried forever on an island the size of a postage stamp, where everyone knew everyone else. It would take two years for the plot to come unglued.

The first domino fell when Melvin Theuma was arrested by Interpol on November 14, 2019, as part of a money-laundering probe into the illegal betting industry. Theuma was connected to loan sharking, horse racing, and possibly narcotics. When he wasn't running illicit financial transactions, he drove a taxi with the rare privilege of operating at the Portomaso complex, home to an office tower and the

Hilton hotel. He was also Portomaso owner Yorgen Fenech's personal driver—but Interpol knew he was involved in so much more. According to island rumor, they'd grown frustrated with the Malta police's refusal to arrest him despite ample evidence. The money-laundering probe would force their hand.

Theuma wasn't in custody long before he started to talk. The small-time crook claimed he had been the middleman in Daphne Caruana Galizia's assassination and promised to testify against the mastermind in exchange for immunity for all his crimes. He was holding an ice cream box tight to his chest and would only open it in the presence of lead investigator Keith Arnaud. It was filled with USB sticks and a photo of himself with Keith Schembri.

He was granted a presidential pardon on the sole authority of Joseph Muscat, but the deal came with conditions. Theuma had to reveal everything he knew, and his testimony had to be corroborated. Did it include avoiding details that would inconvenience the only man with the power to set him free? Like so many other powers in Malta, this one rested with the prime minister. But even Muscat's power couldn't contain a chain reaction that was quickly cascading out of control.

After a week of inaction on the government's part, news media leaked a story claiming the mastermind would soon be revealed and that it was a prominent local businessman. No one was surprised to see Yorgen Fenech cut and run. The AFM intercepted his yacht, *Gio*, as he attempted to flee the country in the predawn hours, forcing him back to the Portomaso marina, where it was boarded, searched, and Fenech placed under arrest.

Thirty-eight-year-old Fenech was the richest man in Malta, heir to a family business empire. His Tumas Group held shares in shipping industries, nightclubs, hotels, and a casino, with assets said to be worth several hundred million euros. Tumas also controlled 30 percent of the Electrogas power station.

Earlier that year Reuters had identified Fenech as the owner of the mysterious Dubai company 17 Black, after tracing cash flows from an Azerbaijani citizen via Latvia's ABLV bank. This information appeared in an intelligence report handed to Malta police by the Financial Intelligence Analysis Unit, but nothing was done despite 17 Black being one of two target clients listed on Keith Schembri and Konrad Mizzi's Panama company incorporation documents.

The businessman must have known the walls were closing in when Melvin Theuma was arrested. When news leaked out that the middleman had been offered a pardon, the alleged mastermind panicked.

Police recovered a surprising amount of data from Fenech's phone, including a conversation with his uncle Ray, who would replace his nephew as head of the Tumas Group.

"There may be developments," Ray said. "Go while you're still in time."

"If I'm caught in the EU, I'll end up at Europol."

"Did you speak to K?" Ray was referring to Keith Schembri, the prime minister's chief of staff.

"Yes, he told me to keep calm. Nothing will happen today."

Yorgen had already signed documents removing himself from the directorship of all Tumas Group companies. He was replaced by his older brother Franco. The two tried arranging a flight with a private pilot on a Falcon jet. "No publicity please," the message read, "we're going to take cash." They were turned down.

"Uncle Ray insists that we gain time," Franco wrote. "We can sort out a way that you can be somewhere safe."

Forget the private jet, Ray told him. They'll be watching the airport. Take your boat and go to France. Catch a flight there, but don't use your credit card. Yorgen asked Uncle Ray to take care of his children.

He planned to travel to Sicily by yacht, while Franco went by ferry. The brothers would continue together to Nice, where a horse trader acquaintance would give them a truck. Using a credit card to rent a car would leave a trail for police to follow, but the men had ample reserves of cash. Apart from the text messages, prosecutors traced "vast amounts of money" being moved from accounts in Dubai and France in the period before Fenech's arrest.

The last person Yorgen called before he tried to make his escape was Keith Schembri. They spoke for twenty-four minutes.

When he was asked whether he would fire Schembri and Mizzi, given their connection to 17 Black, Joseph Muscat said there was nothing pointing toward their involvement in the murder, adding that "the decisions [about the investigation] are not being taken by me." When he was asked about Fenech's dramatic arrest, however, he claimed he had personally ordered increased surveillance after announcing his plan to pardon Theuma. "Had I not done that," he said, "today we might be talking of a person or persons of interest having potentially escaped." Was he meddling in the investigation or wasn't he? He couldn't seem to keep the story straight.

The *Sunday Times of Malta* quoted a former police officer as saying, "This degree of involvement by a prime minister in a criminal investigation is unprecedented, as it was always the police who made announcements regarding the progress or not in such cases." Muscat justified his actions by saying, "I don't want to burden the police with making public announcements on an ongoing and extremely delicate case, so I'm shouldering the responsibility of informing the public." But it was clear he was controlling the narrative.

The stunned silence that had fallen after Fenech's predawn arrest on November 20, 2019, turned to rage as even the most skeptical sycophant began to realize that what Daphne had written was true. All those years of anger—the helpless resentment of the bullied, the frustration of those passed over for promotion because they'd voted for the wrong political party, the bitterness of the person without contacts who watched others cash in—had smoldered since the first scandal broke in 2013, and that accumulated grievance hit a flash point. Enraged citizens filled the square in front of parliament that night, screaming *Barra* (out) and "Mafia." It was the first in a series of increasingly angry nightly protests that would continue into December, bringing the entire country to a halt.

Outrage united groups across the political spectrum. Each clung stubbornly to their own narrative, with Labourites concocting a "stab in the back" by the corrupt inner circle and leftist activists pointing their fingers at "elites," "capitalism," and "big business," but these were just ways of deflecting the blame. The culture of utter corruption from top to bottom was the cause of the current situation. The entire society was responsible for the mire they found themselves in up to their necks, and everyone who benefited or looked away was complicit in Daphne's murder, even if they weren't directly involved in it.

The crowds doubled and then doubled again. Police filled the streets of Valletta, but they were increasingly conflicted between protecting the citizens and defending a regime that clearly had criminal connections. Steel barricades were erected around parliament, transforming Republic Street into a maze of bastions, demibastions, and ravelins, and plainclothes police with Labour connections were spotted photographing protesters. These intimidation tactics were clearly illegal, but they hit home in a country where teachers told students to "keep away from these things because they might take photos at events like these and in future someone might see the photos and recognize you and you might not be given a job because of that." The people responded with air horns and the clatter of metal pots,

disrupting the sitting of a House that had become increasingly illegitimate. They hurled eggs and rotten vegetables at Labour MPs who
attempted to leave, but they were unable to remove a prime minister
whose own office was revealed to be implicated in the assassination of
a journalist who exposed their corruption—and who had been about
to reveal so much more.

The outside world watched in horror as Muscat took on a bunker mentality and his attempts to keep a lid on things began to look
increasingly deranged. The Labour Party rallied the troops for a
counterprotest, as the old guard from the violent 1980s attempted
to mobilize those blind enough to light a candle in front of Joseph's
picture each night. They called for followers to amass in Hamrun
outside party HQ, and from there they would march on Valletta. Police presence was increased, and many feared a repeat of Mintoff-era
violence, but the mobilizing calls circulating on Labour social media
groups went unheeded. They sensed weakness, and no one wanted to
be seen backing the losing side.

When the crisis struck, I changed from filing weekly columns in
*The Shift* to writing multiple articles a day as we tried to collate live
text feeds from our frontline reporters. There were so many protesters
crowding Valletta that our journalists on the scene couldn't upload
photos or video; 4G networks were choked to the breaking point. It
really felt like it was the endgame.

Malta's democracy looked like someone in the last stages of tertiary
syphilis. Every organ had begun to fail, and the brain was increasingly
deranged. Daily life came to a halt, government stopped functioning,
and the economy teetered on the edge of collapse. Order could be re-
stored by removing the prime minister and purging the nation of his
corrupt inner circle, but no one was willing to wield the axe. Instead,
the governing party went into damage control. Cabinet ministers

pointed fingers at one another and tried to distance themselves from Muscat while keeping one foot in the door in case he survived.

The situation was unraveling like a badly knit sweater when Keith Schembri suddenly resigned after a late-night meeting at the prime minister's home on November 25. The chief of staff, the second most powerful man in the country, was arrested the following morning and taken in for questioning while police searched his Mellieħa villa.

A visibly shaken Muscat made the announcement the next morning in a hallway at Castille. His best friend, the chief of staff he had shielded from accountability for three long years, was being interrogated about his role in a political assassination. But did Muscat finally fire him? No. According to the prime minister, "He has now decided to move on." When asked to clarify, he said, "Well, it's a conversation that we have had for some time, and he had already signaled to me that he wanted to move on, and it was a matter of time and when he should move on." When questioned about his own political future, Muscat's criteria for leaving hit an all-time low: "I would definitely resign if there is any sort of association between myself and the murder."

Schembri would not be the last to fall. Konrad Mizzi was forced to resign later that day, reportedly at the insistence of his fellow cabinet members, who feared he would drag them down with his sinking ship. And the economy minister, Chris Cardona, "suspended himself" after being called to police headquarters and questioned. As for Muscat, he survived a vote of confidence in true Stalinist fashion. Despite whispers and "off the record" comments to reporters, not a single minister voted against him. Freshly emboldened by this show of timidity, he vowed to remain in office until he would "see justice served in the murdered journalist's case." But the wave of resignations didn't satisfy protesters who besieged the capital each night. It proved them right and poured petrol on their rage.

Two days after these resignations shocked the country, word leaked out that the cabinet was holding an emergency meeting to decide whether to grant Yorgen Fenech a pardon in exchange for implicating others he claimed were behind the assassination. As protesters gathered in front of the prime minister's office in Castille Square to await the latest developments, Schembri's release was announced by police in a one-line Facebook post: "We investigated Keith Schembri, found no evidence, and released him."

Protesters remained in the square until the marathon six-hour meeting finally ended, and reporters were called in for a press conference. An arrogant Muscat walked to the podium at 3 a.m., with his ministers lined up behind him looking haggard and vaguely ashamed. The pardon had been denied in a decision Muscat claimed had been taken by the entire cabinet after seeking advice from the attorney general. When asked why he had pardoned Theuma but not Fenech, he said the ability to issue pardons did not rest with him alone. It was a direct contradiction of what he had said one week earlier when he claimed he had the unilateral authority to pardon Theuma. Unlike the earlier pardon, the press was told the entire cabinet would bear responsibility for the denial of this one.

No further questions were permitted. The ministers made their escape through a back door while journalists remained locked inside, illegally detained not by police but by a group of thugs dressed in matching black shirts. When asked who they were, one squeaked, "Security services." No one seemed to know who had ordered it. The men had no official position and no official reason for being in the Office of the Prime Minister. They were identified from photographs the next day as Labour Party thugs.

WhatsApp was flooded with rumors as details of the closed-door meeting leaked out. Ministers had been shown a letter in which the chief of staff attempted to frame Economy Minister Chris Cardona for the murder. It had been passed to Fenech by a doctor who visited the alleged mastermind in custody. According to Fenech, Schembri had said, "Don't tell on me and I'll help you." The former chief of staff denied everything. One minister was so upset that he burst into tears. Was he truly shocked, or was he just worried the same could be done to him?

Did Muscat make a deal with Theuma to pin it all on Fenech? Why had Schembri been set free? Were different factions fighting within the police? Did the disgraced former chief of staff really call MP Robert Abela's wife the next day and say, "I know what your husband said about me"? The only thing we knew for sure was that Joseph Muscat was still pulling the strings.

The protests continued. Something had to give. The next act in an increasingly bizarre story took the form of a canned video broadcast on the Labour Party's television station on Sunday evening, December 1. Muscat appeared in a strangely lit room, caked in so much makeup that he looked like he'd been freshly plastered. After a long and rambling account of his many successes, he announced his intention to resign—but not just yet. "I need to shoulder everyone's responsibilities," he said, "even where I am not involved." The nonruler who remained ruler resigned but declared his intention to stay for another five weeks, maintaining his hold on the levers of power. He would limit himself to the day-to-day operations of the government until a new leader was chosen on January 14, 2020. He also decided he was no longer accountable, having told journalists on the steps of Castille that he wouldn't answer any more of their questions because he was no longer prime minister. The man who allegedly participated in the cover-up of a political assassination—possibly even the murder itself—was walking away on his own terms.

Some four thousand people filled the streets around parliament the next day, blockading the disgraced prime minister inside and preventing MPs from leaving. The Nationalist Party members walked out and joined the demonstration, boycotting further sessions of parliament until Muscat stepped down. The air horns and chants and clashing pots went on for two hours. When it was clear that the siege wouldn't be lifted, Muscat scuttled into the basement like a rat, slipping out by a tunnel into the Valletta ditch as his ministers mocked protesters through the window.

In an effort to put an end to the daily protests, Speaker of the House Anglu Farrugia—the same ex-cop who had arrested a young Daphne Caruana Galizia and forced her to sign a false confession—shut down parliament by decree one week before the official 2019 Christmas break. It wouldn't resume until Muscat's successor had been safely installed.

Freed of the obligation to show up in the House, Muscat flew to Rome for a photo with the pope and then jetted off on a seventy-hour "family holiday" to Dubai before returning to Malta and making a quick trip to London. The entire family traveled business class, but no one explained who paid for their tickets or how he could afford this on his declared salary. The rest of his time was spent on a "farewell tour" of minor villages, where he was cheered by adoring red-clad crowds.

After a brief two-person leadership contest, Muscat's chosen successor, Robert Abela, an inexperienced backbench MP who had acted as lawyer and consultant to the prime minister, took power on a mandate of "continuity." Abela's sole rival, Deputy Prime Minister Chris Fearne, had promised he would clean up the rot. He didn't stand a chance.

# TRUTH
# COMES OUT

The details emerged during the compilation of evidence stage in separate court proceedings against the alleged hitmen and the alleged mastermind, and later from the independent public inquiry that Daphne's family fought so hard to get. I sifted through these court reports each week to write a series of seventy-one articles based on this testimony for the Justice for Journalists Foundation on behalf of *The Shift*.

The truth was finally coming out, confirming everything I'd long suspected. But it was worse somehow, reading about what the killers said to each other, how they planned it, how little it cost, and how mundane it all was.

In the months leading up to the 2017 election, Yorgen Fenech called in his regular taxi driver, Melvin Theuma. They met at the Hilton in a lobby next to the Blue Elephant restaurant. "I want to kill Daphne Caruana Galizia," Fenech said. He claimed she was about to reveal something on his uncle Ray, the Tumas group's chairman, and he wanted Theuma to arrange the hit.

The taxi driver went to the Degiorgios' potato shed on the Marsa waterfront the next day. The only question asked in response was, "Does this guy pay?" The price was set a couple days later over coffee at Busy Bee in Msida: €30,000 in advance, and €120,000 when the job was done.

Not long after his meetings, Theuma got a call from Sandro Craus, head of customer care at the Office of the Prime Minister. He was told he had an appointment with Joseph Muscat's chief of staff. "I was taken aback," he said. "I had never been to Castille before." He was met by Keith Schembri, who posed for a photo and ordered coffee before passing the middleman off to Craus. Then the money started to flow. Theuma was paid a monthly salary for a phantom job without ever reporting for work.

Daphne's Egrant allegation, followed by Ali Sadr's midnight run on Pilatus Bank and Muscat's belated request for an inquiry, would briefly disrupt the murder plan, throwing the country into turmoil and purportedly sparking the May 1 snap election call.

Fenech phoned Theuma and told him to "stop everything." Another quick meeting was arranged at Busy Bee, where Degiorgio suspected his gang was being double-crossed. "I hope someone else hasn't been commissioned for the job," he said. But he needn't have worried. The election was held on Saturday, June 3, and the results were clear by Sunday afternoon: an even larger majority for Muscat's Labour government. Fenech called Theuma back that same day. "Get on with it," he said. "I want to kill Daphne."

In the months that followed, an increasingly anxious Fenech hounded the taxi driver with calls, pushing for a quick end to the journalist. "And let's make sure it doesn't end up like Bone's," he said, referring to an earlier gangland car bomb in Msida that had torn both legs off its victim but hadn't killed him.

The Degiorgio brothers and their friend Vince Muscat followed Daphne for months, learning her patterns, which coffee shops she visited, and when she traveled abroad. They watched her house from a secluded spot on the Victoria Lines across the valley from Bidnija using a pair of self-focusing binoculars they'd bought for €300. "I had driven Alfred to Forestals to buy those," hitman Vince Muscat said.

Their vantage point on the abandoned nineteenth-century British defenses provided a perfect view of Daphne's rural home and its surrounding stone wall and carefully tended gardens. "We'd spend long hours there," Vince said, "sometimes from 6 a.m. to nighttime. We'd be sitting there on two bricks. It was uncomfortable, you'd get sore. I'd go get food sometimes. I was buying three packs of Rothmans Reds a day. We disposed of the butts in a water bottle so as not to leave any trace."

They must have seen the family come and go many times, and watched Daphne water her plants or prune trees, perhaps pausing to speak to Toni, the family's elderly Staffordshire terrier. They watched her writing stories on her laptop—"sometimes as late as 2 a.m."—and spotted her car outside a coffee shop in Naxxar, where Vince Muscat went in on the pretext of purchasing a pastry and saw her seated with a laptop. When the family drove to the airport with three large suitcases, the hitmen feared they were "leaving for good," but it was just a vacation.

"One night Alfred and I walked up to her home," Vince said. "The light was on. We saw her seated at her computer; there was a living room. She was doing her work. That seemed to be her study. She was there every day. So we planned for Alfred to shoot her with a telescopic weapon. We had weapons in the car. There was a nine-millimeter automatic that took a sixteen-round magazine and an AK-47 in the car in case we encountered a roadblock."

Listening to Vince Muscat's testimony, son Andrew Caruana Galizia wrote on Twitter: "That August night I took my parents to dinner at the Phoenicia for my mother's 53rd birthday. Newly married, I joked about having children and her becoming a grandmother. She said, 'Isn't that the obvious next step?'"

The killers obtained several rifles and filled sacks with soil to create a makeshift gun rest, but when the time came to carry out the plan, George Degiorgio got cold feet. They opted instead for a tried-and-true Maltese method.

"George always preferred a plan to use a bomb to murder her," Vince Muscat said, because it was "quieter, and causes less panic."

Detectives believe they purchased the SIM cards used in the trigger as early as November 15, 2016. They bought the bomb from Robert Agius (known as Tal-Maksar) and Jamie Vella, career criminals with links to eastern European organized crime. It arrived in September: six inches, "neat," made of stainless steel with five hundred grams of gelignite, a potent explosive made from nitroglycerine and normally used for blasting rock. The device included a place to insert a battery that would last six months and another slot to insert a SIM card. Worried that the explosion would maim their target rather than kill, the men attached a small bottle of petrol to the device to improve its effectiveness. Agius and Vella told the killers to place it under the driver's seat of Daphne's car. They also procured a rental car that was exactly the same as the Peugeot 107 Daphne drove, so the killers could practice picking the lock.

Then they settled in to wait. Discarded cigarette butts piled up near the wall that was used as a lookout. As the summer wore on and the thermometer climbed toward 40 degrees Celsius, the killers were pressured to get the job done.

"Whoever it was wanted to hurry things up," Vince said. "Melvin Theuma used to tell Alfred, and I was with Alfred every day."

"She's giving us problems, but she'll get it," Degiorgio replied. "A lot of tough guys have died. She will die too."

They decided in early October to strike when Daphne drove home from the popular Notte Bianca festival. "We expected her to attend. Everyone went there. Not that we would blow it up amidst people.

We'd do it as she drove home." As they drove through Floriana, Vince recalls the Degiorgios saying they didn't care who else was with her in the car that night. "Whoever it is, it could be her children," they said. One night they realized her car had been parked outside the gate of her home. "Some days after Notte Bianca, on October 15 at around 9 p.m., I was going out to eat with my partner," Vince said. "Alfred called up on the burner phone and said, 'Cens, her car is outside.' I wasn't pleased. I was going out to eat with my family. It was around 9 p.m., late. I told him the bomb was in Saint Venera, so he said, 'So just bring it down here!' And I had to take it down there like an idiot."

George manned the lookout post at the Tarġa Battery while Vince watched the lane. "Fredu opened the car with his device," Vince said, "the same we did it when practicing. He opened the rear door and placed the bomb under the seat and switched it on." The SIM card attached to the trigger was switched on at 1:41 a.m. "Then we went away on foot back to the reservoir. We waited for George, but he had gone home. First we spent an hour there looking for movement. I went with Alfred back to the flat. He wanted me to stay on, just in case he oversleeps or something."

The next morning dawned hot and still, with intense October sun streaming down on the green fields of Bidnija. "At 6 a.m. we were already in position," Vince said. George told friends he was going fishing. He took his boat, *Maya*, outside the mouth of the Grand Harbour at 7:55 a.m. and headed northwest. "George had to go far out to sea, as far out as possible. I can't recall the name of the boat but knew its color, white and blue. We got an umbrella with us, just in case of rain, and made a position for us to wait for Caruana Galizia to leave in her car. A lot of time had passed. George called to ask what was happening."

He was recorded by the security services, which had been tapping his phone for months because they suspected him of being involved in other unspecified crimes. He had his normal phone with him, along with the burner phone the killers were using solely for the hit. That mistake would allow investigators to reconstruct his movements.

Daphne published her last story around 3 p.m.—the one about Keith Schembri that ended, "There are crooks everywhere you look now. The situation is desperate." Then she grabbed her purse and left the house to drive to the bank. Alfred Degiorgio called his brother George but quickly disconnected when he saw her go back inside. She had forgotten her checkbook. "Okay, now I really am going," she said to her son Matthew. She left home at 2:55 p.m., just as George Degiorgio was passing the Grand Harbour breakwater in the *Maya* on his way back to Marsa.

Alfred called again, this time for nearly two minutes. George hit "send" on the trigger phone while they sat on the line. He must have heard the explosion through his brother's phone when his text message—#REL1=ON—detonated the bomb. And then he started the *Maya*'s engine and headed back to the potato shed. He called a friend with his regular phone on the way—the phone the security services were listening to—and said, "I caught two big fish today." He was laughing. At 3:30 p.m. he sent a text to his wife that read "Open a bottle of wine for me, baby."

After confirming that the job was done, Vince Muscat went to Rabat for a cup of tea, just as he'd gone to Hamrun for a kebab when they received the initial deposit for the murder.

Less than two weeks later Theuma met Alfred Degiorgio at Ramla Taz-Zejtun and handed him €120,000 in elastic-wrapped bundles of €50 notes, plus another €5,000 to cover the cost of rental cars and the binoculars. He made it all sound so matter-of-fact, just another routine job on an island where car bombs were used to settle scores. That was simply the price of a life.

It was difficult to imagine these scenes playing out in a setting I knew so well. I had eaten at the Blue Elephant many times with my wife. We'd gone with Marian, and we took Tomoko's parents there twice when they visited Malta. The spot near the Tarġa Battery where the killers watched Daphne's home was a stone's throw from our penthouse in Mosta. Melvin Theuma lived in Zurrieq, near our last flat. We'd taken coffee at Busy Bee in Msida and spent our first island years in the Zejtun palazzo, not far from where the killers were paid off. How many times had we brushed past such people or sat near them in a restaurant? Criminality isn't a distant abstraction on an island as small as Malta. Sometimes it's the man who lives down the street.

Yorgen Fenech was worried about the monthly vigils and the protest memorial that refused to go away, but he told Theuma they'd be safe as long as Labour retained power. For the three years after Daphne was killed, this proved to be true.

According to the accused mastermind, he, Keith Schembri, and Joseph Muscat "were like brothers." Police found lengthy WhatsApp chats with the former prime minister on Fenech's mobile. He gave Muscat a limited-edition Bulgari watch worth some €20,000 and attended his booze-fueled private birthday party in the former chapel of Girgenti palace, a country retreat for the serving prime minister— an event not even cabinet ministers were invited to—where he gave Muscat a rare bottle of Petrus wine vintage 1974, the year of his birth, worth thousands of euros. It took place after the prime minister had been informed by police that Fenech was a suspect. The party caused a minor scandal when a video was posted on social media showing the Muscats clutching a bottle of champagne, jumping up and down, and singing along to the words "You can't touch our Joseph!"

Fenech claimed Muscat had spoken to him twice about the mur-der. First at Castille, the building that houses the Office of the Prime

Minister, where Muscat asked him if he trusted middleman Melvin
Theuma. "Not really," Fenech replied, "because he's recording me."
Fenech also claimed that Muscat warned him in summer 2019 that
police were planning a raid on Theuma.

The owner of 17 Black had a similar close relationship with Keith
Schembri. The two sent each other selfies and chatted about recipes
on WhatsApp. The former chief of staff was given a white-gold watch
for his fortieth birthday, a trinket worth some €12,000. Fenech and
Schembri vacationed together multiple times, and Fenech picked up
the tab for Schembri's cancer treatments in the United States. Muscat,
Schembri, and Fenech also attended Pilatus Bank owner Ali Sadr's
small private wedding in Florence in 2015, all expenses paid.

These weren't the only ties between the corrupt businessman
and the seat of power. Deputy Police Commissioner Silvio Valletta
was keeping Schembri informed of his investigation into Daphne's
murder, and that information was being leaked to Yorgen Fenech.
Schembri told the businessman his phone was tapped, and it would
be better if he "stays careful."

"[Fenech] trusted Keith Schembri more than Silvio Valletta," Melvin Theuma told the courts. "In fact, Yorgen once told me that he
would not tell Valletta the whole truth unless strictly necessary."

Valletta would be removed from the case at the insistence of the
Caruana Galizia family because the country's second most powerful
cop was married to a prominent Labour minister, but his conflicts of
interest didn't end in the bedroom. The chief investigator vacationed
with Fenech on his yacht in September 2018, at a time when the businessman was already the lead suspect. The top cop and the businessman were so close that Yorgen's children called him Uncle Silvio.

As rumors leaked out that one of the hitmen had begun talking to
police, Melvin Theuma became increasingly suspicious that Fenech
was planning to "put him away or kill him." He was the only direct

link between the businessman and the men who planted the bomb. He recalled an incident when Fenech had given him a large piece of meat and a bottle of wine. Theuma called his partner to tell her he planned to throw it away on his way home in case it was poisoned. He claims Fenech confronted him about it a few days later. "Who told Fenech? My partner? I don't think so!"

The taxi driver began recording their conversations using a hidden phone set to airplane mode as a form of insurance. The ice cream box filled with USB sticks that he handed to police revealed just how deep the cover-up had gone.

Theuma's concerns were lent some validity by testimony from Counter Terrorism Unit head George Cremona, who was contacted by U.S. Homeland Security agents investigating a case where firearms, ammunition, and a silencer were purchased on the dark web, to be delivered to "George Fenech, 21st floor Portomaso, St. Julians." U.S. investigators had also traced online searches for the deadly poison ricin back to a device owned by Fenech.

It wasn't the first time the businessman had tried to buy himself an arsenal. Days after Reuters outed him as the owner of 17 Black in November 2018, Fenech attempted to buy two grenades, a Glock pistol and silencer, two Scorpion submachine guns, and eight hundred rounds of ammunition on the dark web using five different cryptocurrency wallets. He also received an email stating that a twenty-gram shipment of potassium cyanide had been sent to him that morning. In April 2019 he tried to procure one gram of potassium cyanide for $2,098, employing a username and password to access dark web pages for the potential purchase of enough poison to kill an adult male weighing eighty kilograms. These events took place in the period when they knew Theuma was going to be arrested.

Thanks to his police connections, Fenech was able to give Melvin Theuma advance warning that he was about to be investigated for money laundering. Make "100 percent sure everywhere is clean," Fenech told him before the police carried out their raid.

Theuma asked Yorgen to speak to "the hotshot from Luqa"—Police Commissioner Lawrence Cutajar—so he could keep his partner and daughter out of it. "Fight this, if need be," he said. "There should be a bit more time so it doesn't take place this Saturday, so everyone can keep going on with their lives." Yorgen told him not to worry. "Ray" would be carrying out the arrest. Theuma would just be questioned and released.

In another recording, Fenech's business associate Johann Cremona promises the taxi driver and part-time loan shark that he would be forewarned about places the police intended to search. "Don't forget that these guys are with you," Cremona said. "The police and the prime minister, they're all with you. If you get Raymond, then I don't know who else you need." They were referring to inspector Raymond Aquilina of the economic crimes squad.

The arrest was planned for November 16, but police moved two days earlier after they learned Theuma had been tipped off. They also showed up without "Ray." When the taxi driver realized that he wasn't going to be released as planned, he tried to buy his way out by spilling what he knew about the assassination.

When asked by the court if he still considered Yorgen Fenech a friend, the middleman replied, "Yes, before. Not now. He's the worst man in Malta—in the whole world—because he got me into this mess."

Caruana Galizia family lawyer Jason Azzopardi stepped in. "How do you feel having murdered a woman and mother?"

"At 3 p.m. on October 16, 2017, my life ended."

"Daphne Caruana Galizia lost her life," the lawyer said.

"And I as much as her."

# BOMB-MAKING
# BROTHERS

The bomb makers would only be hauled in after Vince Muscat turned state's witness in February 2021. The hitman was given a fifteen-year sentence plus a bill for €40,000 in court expenses in a plea-bargain deal that saw him provide information on Daphne's murder and on the unrelated contract killing of a lawyer, allegedly over a loan gone bad. The sudden change was an unexpected twist in proceedings that had dragged on for more than three years.

The case against Vince Muscat and the Degiorgio brothers was based on hard evidence from FBI and Europol experts, who traced the killers' movements by meticulous analysis of cell phone data in the days and hours leading up to Daphne's murder. Vince was unlikely to offer prosecutors new evidence against Yorgen Fenech. Melvin Theuma was the buffer between the businessman and the hitmen, and he was already testifying against both—again, in exchange for a presidential pardon absolving him of responsibility for his crimes.

Adrian and Robert Agius, and their associate Jamie Vella, had already been named by Theuma more than two years earlier in the compilation of evidence against Fenech. They were among the ten men arrested in the same December 2017 police raid that led to the capture of the three hitmen, but they were released without charge in less than forty-eight hours. They were not called in again.

The so called Tal-Maksar brothers' intimate connections to organized crime, drug trafficking, smuggling, and a series of car bomb killings that played out over the previous decade were common knowledge. Their father, Raymond Agius, was a suspected contraband cigarette smuggler with interests in construction and a car dealership. He was shot twice in the head in 2008 by two assailants wearing motorcycle helmets at a bar in central Malta. The murder remains unsolved but is believed to have been a hit ordered by a rival smuggler.

Three years later one of the island's major traffickers was robbed of twenty kilos of cocaine, sparking off a spree of professional hits that created a vacuum in Malta's smuggling world that would be filled by Robert and Adrian. Their rise to prominence coincided with a series of murders and attempted murders by car bomb. All were carried out in broad daylight in busy commuter traffic, and all remained unsolved.

Robert Agius did have one brush with the law. He was arraigned in 2012 and charged with heroin trafficking, but the case fell apart when the main witness—a woman referred to as an "exploited drug mule" by judge Edwina Grima—failed to testify. She had already given sworn testimony during a magisterial inquiry into the drug bust, but it was discarded on the basis of case law that required her to testify again viva voce to allow the defense to cross-examine her. It should have been an open-and-shut case. Agius had been caught on tape receiving drugs in a controlled delivery set up by police, but the court declared that the prosecution had not sufficiently proved the accused's intention to sell or traffic. As for the charge of cocaine possession, the substance had never been scientifically analyzed by police, so they failed to prove it was an illegal drug. Was the case deliberately sabotaged, or were the police simply incompetent? In the end Robert Agius was charged with possession of a live bullet and fined €500. The court also ruled that his rights had been breached because the case had taken too long to conclude.

Though middleman-turned-state's-witness Melvin Theuma claims he'd never heard of Tal-Maksar, he testified that Fenech told him in 2018 to put pressure on the men who supplied the bomb. The press also revealed that Agius and Jamie Vella had approached a relative of Vince Muscat's in 2019, allegedly offering the family €1,500 a month in exchange for the accused hitman's silence. Most alarming of all, police found a photo from a classified intelligence report about the criminal gang on Yorgen Fenech's phone. Such documents could only have come from someone at the highest level of government.

How could the Tal-Maksar brothers operate with total impunity when their connections to organized crime were common knowledge? And why did the institutions wait so long to reel them in?

Prime minister Robert Abela, a lawyer by profession, had personally represented the Agius brothers in court in 2012 and 2016, before he was chosen as Joseph Muscat's successor, and yet he decided not to recuse himself from cabinet-level discussions of Vince Muscat's pardon requests, insisting there was no conflict of interest. The hitman later tried to negotiate pardons for three more crimes, one of which allegedly involved a former government minister and a sitting politician.

Despite Abela's insistence that investigators had no evidence indicating that a politician was involved in Daphne's murder, the *Times of Malta* published a story the next day claiming Vince Muscat had told police that Chris Cardona, the former economy minister, had hatched a separate plot to kill Daphne in 2015. Muscat would eventually claim in court in March 2021 that the plot did not go ahead because Cardona's associate David Gatt failed to pay the Degiorgio brothers the agreed-upon deposit.

Vince told the court how he'd staked out Caruana Galizia's home in 2015 and identified her car close to the building of the *Malta Independent*, where she was working as a columnist. "George and I spent around three days watching her," he said, and then they came up with a plan. "Once she exited her house down the valley, George and Jamie would block her path and Jamie would machine-gun her. We already had an AK-47; we got it from abroad."

Asked by lawyer Jason Azzopardi if they were worried that the economy minister would expose the plot, Vince said, "We knew each other already so we were sure he would help out." Besides, Cardona had been involved in another crime they carried out years earlier with another minister. The career criminal's reference to a "big job" sparked media speculation that he was describing a botched 2010 HSBC bank heist in the village of Qormi, where minister Carmelo Abela was manager at the time. Despite these alarming allegations, Abela refused to ask his cabinet if the hitman-turned-state's-witness was referring to one of them.

The same names came up again and again in connection to the corruption that led to Daphne's murder.

Yorgen Fenech hadn't been under interrogation for more than two days when he was taken to hospital with chest pains. The police summoned his personal doctor. When Adrian Vella arrived to examine him, he was carrying a message from Keith Schembri.

Dr. Vella told the court that Schembri had called him early that Sunday and asked him to stop by his house in Mellieħa, in the north of the island. Vella chatted with the chief of staff's wife for about twenty minutes. Then Schembri came down the stairs leading to the living room, pointed at some papers on his desk, and said, "Take these. Give them to Yorgen Fenech."

The letter the doctor smuggled to Fenech was the same document shown to ministers during Joseph Muscat's all-night cabinet meeting, with the plan to pin the journalist's murder on former economy minister Chris Cardona. The scenario seemed plausible enough. Cardona had frozen Daphne's bank account as part of a massive libel suit, and he had been seen with the hitmen who planted the bomb in her car. The island's gossip network had already flagged him as a suspect. But the cumbersome series of explanations Schembri allegedly wrote for Fenech to memorize read like the sort of excuse a primary school child comes up with to avoid detention.

When Vella passed the folded A4 papers to Fenech, the accused mastermind looked at them and said, "If I go down, everyone goes down with me." Not "he goes down with me," as in Schembri, but "everyone goes down with me."

The accused mastermind gave police four statements when he learned that his request for a pardon had been denied. He said it was Schembri who told him to "find someone to kill Daphne Caruana Galizia." The former prime minister's chief of staff brought it up multiple times, both directly and indirectly, as far back as 2014. Keith "wanted to get rid of" the journalist, Fenech said, because "she was a lot of trouble." And he wanted Fenech to finance the assassination.

When Fenech told him he'd found hitmen to do the job for €120,000, the former chief of staff replied, "*Mexxi mexxi mexxi*" (Go ahead). Schembri also contributed €85,000 to middleman Melvin Theuma in connection with the killing.

"There were three persons who knew this after the murder," Fenech told police. "Joseph Muscat, Adrian Vella, and Johann Cremona."

It wasn't the only version of events when it came to political connections. Hitman Vince Muscat said under oath that Schembri and former economy minister Chris Cardona knew about the plot prior to it being executed, and that former deputy police commissioner Silvio Valletta had given the killers information on Daphne's whereabouts.

When asked about *The Shift*'s report of an incident where Joseph Muscat had turned pale and fainted at an event two days prior to the assassination, Cardona claimed Muscat simply hadn't eaten anything that day and he didn't know why the public was kept uninformed.

A member of the prime minister's security detail, Kenneth Camilleri, also admitted to police that Schembri had sent him to "calm down" Melvin Theuma in 2018 when the middleman was urging those involved to help the hitmen obtain bail. Camilleri said he had "no idea" the meeting was linked to Daphne's murder, adding that Schembri later told him not to approach Theuma anymore. His admission contradicted what he'd told police under questioning in the wake of Fenech's arrest, when Joseph Muscat was still clinging to power amidst widespread protests.

Yorgen Fenech's phone would provide investigators with a treasure trove of information that cast doubt on the former prime minister's attempt to distance himself from the accused murder mastermind. Chief Inspector Keith Arnaud told the court that it was Joseph Muscat who set up the infamous WhatsApp group with Fenech and Schembri two days after the alleged hitmen were arrested. Muscat claimed he hadn't spoken to Fenech for at least a year before the businessman's arrest. And yet Arnaud drew the court's attention to one particular message that said, "we need to talk, you, me and k," sent in January 2019 before the men met at Muscat's private birthday party. The prime minister only removed himself from the chat when the *Times of Malta* leaked news that "a major businessman" was among the main suspects in the assassination.

Fenech's relationship with Schembri was even closer. The two were part of another private chat group that included Joseph Cuschieri, former CEO of Malta's financial services regulator, and the deputy police commissioner, Silvio Valletta, who was lead investigator in the murder case at the time. Investigators found a copy of the draft presidential pardon offered to middleman Melvin Theuma on Fenech's phone. He told police it was sent to him by Schembri, but police claim they couldn't confirm this because Schembri "lost" his phone hours before his brief November 2019 arrest. Fenech told police Schembri called him "at least thirty times" on the day Melvin Theuma was arrested. They also extracted messages that Fenech sent to Schembri the night before his dramatic predawn escape attempt, including "Don't leave me alone." Fenech asked if "they were going to come today," to which Schembri replied, "No."

Despite these damning political connections, so much of the case against Yorgen Fenech depended on Melvin Theuma and his secret recordings. In July 2020, the night before he was due to testify, the middleman-turned-state's-witness was found with a slit throat and a further six stab wounds to his abdomen as well as cuts to his wrist. He was under police protection at the time. Medical practitioners at Mater Dei hospital told *The Shift* on condition of anonymity, "His neck was in two pieces. The bottom of the thyroid was hanging loose. His jugular vein was severed." His airway was punctured, and he could not speak. Photos taken that night—and seen by the *Guardian*—show a plate of pasta sitting untouched on the kitchen table. There were trails of blood in the bedroom but no obvious signs of struggle. Both the police and Theuma insisted the injuries were self-inflicted, despite wounds that would have sent any normal individual into shock, likely to the point of unconsciousness, rather than allow him to continue stabbing himself in a frantic bid to end his own life.

The witness survived, but the defense team made constant attempts to damage his credibility, aided by lawyer Charles Mercieca, who joined Yorgen Fenech's legal team within twenty-four hours of resigning from the attorney general's office, a move that prompted accusations of collusion.

The entire story is a tangled web of deliberate inaction on the part of police, political interference in the murder investigation, endless court delays caused by legal haranguing, and cover-ups that could only have originated at the highest levels of government.

As long as those involved could remain in control—and keep things safely contained within Malta—they still had a chance of weathering the storm.

FIVE

# THE WAGES

# OF SIN

# EVERYONE WAS ON
# THE TAKE

At the time of her death, Daphne Caruana Galizia had been working through a massive collection of some 600,000 documents from the Electrogas power station that had been leaked to her by a whistleblower. Her son Matthew claimed it contained information that would have brought down the government. The project that was the Labour Party's biggest pre-election promise "bled half a billion euros in three years," he wrote on social media. "It couldn't even pay its employees, or even [for] a cup of coffee, because one of its creditors garnisheed its bank account. It wasn't generating electricity, and SOCAR was invoicing it for millions of euros."

Its bank balance had shrunk from €450 million to just €100,000 by February 2017. On September 4, the Bank of Valletta notified the Maltese government that Electrogas was bankrupt. How long before Daphne revealed this, scaring off the foreign financing they so desperately needed to pull their Roadmap to Personal Riches through?

Muscat's government forced the island's banks to guarantee a massive bridge loan of €360 million to make sure Electrogas stayed above water. Daphne was murdered on October 16, 2017. Twelve days later Konrad Mizzi bypassed the cabinet and unilaterally wrote off the entity's tax responsibilities, not just the accrual but for the full eighteen

years, quietly sticking Maltese citizens with more than €40 million
in excise dues that the fledgling energy consortium couldn't pay—at
least, not without cutting into their profits.

On December 15 Mizzi and Yorgen Fenech signed a security of
supply agreement on behalf of Malta and Electrogas in an effort to
convince international banks to extend the embattled energy company loans. Internal Electrogas emails show Fenech insisting that the
agreement not be shared with anyone—including the banks they
hoped would put up more cash. "The government (GOM) said that
under no circumstances it is true [sic] that the government would
allow the LNG [liquefied natural gas] Security of Supply Agreement
(SSA) to be divulged to the lenders," he wrote.

One email from a London-based lawyer for the banks revealed
how frustrated they were by this secrecy. "Our concern, which we
have expressed to [Electrogas] on several occasions, is that the LNG
[security of supply agreement] may contain elements of State Aid
which should have been disclosed to the [European] Commission."
They did finally get access to the agreement, but they had to fly to
Geneva for a private viewing, with government and SOCAR representatives present. The lawyers insisted the dodgy agreement be
terminated before the international banks would lend Electrogas any
more cash.

With this roadblock out of the way, the European Commission
went on to approve state aid for Mizzi and Fenech's pet project without ever finding out about the secret side deal that obligated Electrogas to buy liquefied natural gas from Azerbaijan's SOCAR at inflated
prices for a period of eighteen years. The government's loan guarantee
could finally be withdrawn.

It had been a desperate risk to take. "If my mother had published
the Electrogas leak we were working on," Matthew wrote, "and had
revealed the fact that 17 Black is owned by the director of Electrogas,

and that it had promised a bribe to the Minister of Energy, then Electrogas would have failed the compliance test by the banks." The company would have gone into liquidation, and the default on its loans would have triggered a collapse of the government's credit rating, because the country was on the hook for the astronomical debts of a private company. Faced with skyrocketing interest rates on its other loans, Malta risked being reduced to Argentine status, a bankrupt nation without a power station, from "Best in Europe" to "IMF basket case" in just four years. "What greater motive would the people involved need to commit murder?" Matthew wrote.

The data leak would eventually reveal that the web of corruption extended well beyond Fenech's Tumas Group of companies.

Another UAE company was set up at the same time as Konrad Mizzi's and Keith Schembri's Panama entities. Kittiwake Limited, owned by fellow Electrogas director Paul Apap Bologna, was a carbon copy of Fenech's 17 Black. Apap Bologna was the scion of one of Malta's "noble" families and a key investor in the project, along with the Gasan family and the Fenech family's Tumas Group. An extra 10 percent was also owned by Yorgen individually. Together they formed the 33 percent of Electrogas owned by GEM Holdings.

When asked to explain this arrangement in front of a parliamentary committee, Apap Bologna said the group had agreed to let Fenech hold the extra 10 percent after discussion with Yorgen's late father, George. He changed his story in time for the next hearing, claiming the 10 percent stake was Yorgen's from the beginning because he had taken the lead in the project. Why Fenech held those shares in his personal capacity rather than folding them into Tumas Energy's investment, no one seemed to know. Suspicions were raised that this 10 percent could have been the source of the €5,000 per day that Keith Schembri's and Konrad Mizzi's Panama companies were expecting to receive as kickbacks.

A leaked report from Malta's Financial Intelligence Analysis Unit said Fenech's 17 Black was paid €161,000 from a local Maltese agent for the floating liquefied natural gas storage tanker that supplied the power station, as well as two separate payments that totaled €1.1 million from a Seychelles-registered company owned—at least on paper—by a fifty-one-year-old Azerbaijani citizen described as a "former subway worker."

Fenech didn't waste any time covering his tracks when the mysterious name 17 Black popped up in the Panama Papers. It was now called Wings Investment. Paul Apap Bologna's Kittiwake transferred $200,000 to Wings Investment days before Daphne first mentioned 17 Black and speculated about the identity of its beneficial owner. Another company, EN3 Projects, sent $300,000 to Wings Investments at around the same time. When his bank in the UAE asked for details, Fenech told them he was doing business with EN3 Projects in Qatar and Bangladesh—with help from Kittiwake owner Paul Apap Bologna. It was a direct contradiction of Apap Bologna's sworn testimony; he claimed he had only found out from the press that Fenech was planning to replicate the Electrogas project in Bangladesh.

It wasn't the first time Apap Bologna's credibility had been cast into doubt. When asked under oath if he had questioned Fenech about the reason for the latter's sudden resignation as Electrogas director just days before his dramatic escape attempt and arrest, he said, "I didn't speak to Fenech."

"Be careful," lawyer Jason Azzopardi warned him, "mobile data concerning Yorgen Fenech will be coming out."

"I may have spoken to him," Apap Bologna replied.

The existence of Kittiwake Limited is a clear indication that Apap Bologna was in on the deal from the beginning, but he has not been questioned by police.

As for the Gasan Group—Apap Bologna's fellow shareholders—

they issued a statement in October 2020 saying: "We have not received any dividends and have only registered losses in relation to our investment in Electrogas." Apap Bologna chimed in too, claiming he was only expecting to see a profit in either 2023 or "the end of the decade."

Yet investigations by the press revealed that the conglomerate of shareholders controlling the project paid themselves more than €16 million in "success fees" out of loans granted to Electrogas on the back of the last-minute multimillion-euro state guarantee. Despite the amount of money on the table—and the sizable investment made by his business—Apap Bologna claimed he "didn't know" how, out of the millions in development costs, €20 million were allocated to development fees, success fees, and rebates for shareholders.

Yorgen Fenech's 17 Black wasn't the only source of funding for Mizzi's and Schembri's illicit Panama companies. An offshore structure, called Macbridge, was also named in leaked incorporation documents as their other intended source of income.

A joint yearlong investigation by Reuters and the *Times of Malta* tracked down Macbridge's beneficial owner: Tang Zhaomin, the mother-in-law of Accenture negotiator Chen Cheng, the consultant who played a key role in Shanghai Electric Power's involvement in two controversial deals—a 33 percent investment in state-owned Enemalta and a corrupt wind farm deal in Montenegro.

Shanghai Electric paid €100 million for its 33 percent stake in Enemalta and €150 million for a 90 percent share in the BWSC power plant on the Delimara peninsula. The Chinese company would also spend €70 million to convert the BWSC plant from running on heavy fuel oil to gas. In return, Malta was obliged to buy back energy from Shanghai Electric. Konrad Mizzi and Joseph Muscat pitched the March 2014 announcement as a €320 million investment in the country; in reality, Shanghai Electric was making €41,000 a day sell-ing energy back to Enemalta. The BWSC station was producing just 28 percent of Malta's electricity at a rate two times higher than that charged by the more stable Sicily interconnector.

The new cash injection from China allowed Enemalta to make its first overseas investment: a wind farm in Montenegro, bought for €10.3 million in a deal brokered by Mizzi. As with everything else the Panama Papers minister touched, all was not as it appeared on the surface.

An investigation by Reuters and the *Times of Malta* revealed that Cifidex, a Seychelles-registered company, had signed a promise of sale agreement in February 2015 to buy a 99 percent share in the wind farm for just €2.9 million. The other 1 percent would be held by a Montenegrin company. The deal went through in December 2015. Two weeks later Cifidex sold its shares to Enemalta for €10.3 million.

Cifidex was owned by Turab Musayev, an Azerbaijani national who was just a bit player before Labour's 2013 election victory. Back then, he ran SOCAR Trading (STSA), a Switzerland-based oil-trading company that dealt in Azerbaijani crude. He got into the liquefied natural gas business when Malta chose the Electrogas consortium to run its new power station. Under the dodgy security-of-supply contract Mizzi signed on behalf of Malta, Musayev's STSA bought liquefied natural gas from Shell, who bought it from Trinidad & To-bago and Nigeria. STSA then turned around and sold that same gas to Electrogas at a $40 million a year markup.

Yorgen Fenech's 17 Black loaned Musayev's Cifidex the €2.9 million it needed to buy the Montenegrin wind farm. When the €10.3 million deal with Enemalta went through, Musayev paid back Fenech's loan plus an additional €4.6 million, leaving Cifidex with a tidy €2.8 million profit.

It was another variation on the Electrogas template, but this time

EVERYONE WAS ON THE TAKE

the Montenegrins were being sold out, contracted to buy electricity from the wind farm at three times the market price. Montenegro touted it as investment by a European Union member state, but Enemalta was controlled by the Chinese state, which soon transferred the project to a China-dominated consortium linked to the totalitarian state's "belt and road" initiative.

When Reuters and the *Times of Malta* tracked down Macbridge's owner, they found corporate filings in Hong Kong that revealed the existence of yet another company, Dow's Media, owned by the business partner of Chen Cheng's mother-in-law and registered at the same time as Macbridge. Dow's Media received €1 million from 17 Black in 2016 after Fenech's company reaped its €4.6 million profit from the wind farm deal that Chen had helped negotiate with Enemalta. Macbridge and Dow's Media were dissolved within a week of each other after Fenech was exposed as the owner of 17 Black.

Not long before the wind farm scandal broke, Joseph Muscat had made Karl Izzo ambassador to Montenegro. When he was asked what qualified him for this post, apart from being a close personal friend of the prime minister, the former national water polo coach referred to his many trips to the small Balkan country. "What's wrong with being the friend of the prime minister?" he added. "He is my friend. I don't need any favors from anyone. I built my business from the ground up, everyone knows the type of person I am....I am an honest man." The prime minister also appointed Yorgen Fenech's cousin Matthew as honorary consul to nearby North Macedonia.

Muscat's last foreign visit as prime minister, before he was forced to resign in disgrace for his administration's ties to Daphne's murder, was to Montenegro on November 18, 2019, where he joined Prime Minister Duško Marković to cut the ribbon on the wind farm built with Maltese money. Two days later Yorgen Fenech would be arrested while attempting to flee Malta on his yacht.

And what of the Bangladesh connection that reportedly involved Fenech's fellow Electrogas director Paul Apap Bologna? Yorgen and his brother Franco flew to Bangladesh in October 2015—three months after Konrad Mizzi's and Keith Schembri's New Zealand trusts went live—plastering a trail of photos all over Franco's Instagram page. Franco said their visit to one of the world's most overcrowded countries had "exceeded his expectations."

Two months later, in December 2015, Karl Cini of the accounting firm NexiaBT amended Keith Schembri's and Konrad Mizzi's Panama company documents to add three more items to the list of businesses they would be involved in, this time in the Indian subcontinent: infrastructure projects, maritime and fisheries, and tourism. Quite a broad mix for two guys who were supposed to be busy running a country. Cini wasn't sure if they would be paid through shareholder dividends or straight-up fees, but he knew the main source of incoming funds would be 17 Black and Macbridge.

Where would 17 Black get the money to pay the two Maltese government officials? That's where Fenech's Azerbaijani friend Turab Musayev came in. The two were already working together on the power station project and the wind farm deal. Musayev's company STSA used the "successful" Electrogas project in Malta—a European Union country—to pitch the same scheme to delegations from Qatar, Kenya, Namibia, the Ivory Coast, and Bangladesh.

Fenech knew even the best-laid plans would fail without a greedy collaborator inside the government who was willing to put his own interests above those of the nation. Cue Salman Rahman, a senior adviser to Bangladesh's prime minister and co-owner of the Beximco Group, a conglomerate with interests in pharmaceuticals, aquaculture, textiles, ceramics, energy, media, and financial services. It isn't known how the two hooked up. Some say Yorgen's brother met Rahman in rehab. What matters is that Bangladesh was conducting a revision of its Energy Master Plan at the time, and Rahman knew the intimate details. Yorgen had found his Bangladeshi Schembri.

By February 2016 Fenech was paying a Dutch energy consulting firm to design an "energy hub" for Bangladesh that featured a liquefied petroleum gas facility and a liquefied natural gas plant. The details read like a carbon copy of Electrogas, right down to the "storm mooring" system and the 600 to 1000 MWh generating capacity. The Dutch company was even promised the project designs from Malta to make copying easier.

By late 2016 the Tumas Group and Rahman's Beximco were talking joint venture. Fenech sent Electrogas director Catherine Halpin an email from Bangladesh asking for photos of Malta's power station for him and Turab Musayev to use in their presentation.

Just as sure as Konrad Mizzi's insider-packed evaluation committee recommended Electrogas, Bangladesh decided it needed to import liquefied natural gas to generate power too. The Tumas Group and Beximco signed a memorandum of understanding with the Bangladeshi Ministry for Energy and Petrobangla in February 2017.

It's not clear what Fenech was supposed to bring to this project beyond the carbon copy plan or who else would cash in. 17 Black's links to Azerbaijani money and Schembri's "draft business plans" suggest that he was backed by those in power. But even copy-and-paste can go wrong. Bangladesh eventually ditched the floating tanker idea, and Rahman cut his Maltese "friend" out of the loop. The company failed, and the whole thing vanished without a trace. Even the memorandum of understanding disappeared. Rahman would try to go it alone again as recently as July 2019, this time without any help from the Tumas Group.

Caruana Galizia murder middleman Melvin Theuma recalled Fenech telling him, "I did everything with precision for the power station. This [the murder] is the last thing I need. I'm feeling trapped between four walls."

Lead inspector Kurt Zahra confirmed that police believed Daphne was killed "because of something she was going to release, not because of something she had already written about." The threads revealed by the massive trove of Electrogas data leaked to the slain journalist exposed a network of corruption that extends beyond Malta and beyond the Mediterranean.

As of 2023, more than six years after Daphne's death, the Maltese police have not opened credible investigations into Electrogas or any other government deal involving Yorgen Fenech.

# THE
# PUBLIC INQUIRY

The conspirators thought killing the one investigative journalist who threatened their plan would make their problems go away. Instead, it brought the attention of the world.

Malta became the first European Union member state to be subjected to the scrutiny of a special rapporteur from the Parliamentary Assembly of the Council of Europe, which gave its full support to Pieter Omtzigt's call for an independent public inquiry to be conducted in Malta, independent of state authorities, tasked with determining whether the state facilitated Daphne's murder or failed to prevent it. The inquiry had to begin within three months of the council's June 26, 2019, resolution.

The Maltese government did everything it could to resist its obligation under Article 2 of the European Convention on Human Rights, insisting an inquiry would jeopardize the criminal proceedings then under way against the accused hitmen. The Council of Europe responded with an ultimatum, warning that "Malta's weaknesses are a source of vulnerability for all of Europe." If "Malta cannot or will not correct its weaknesses, European institutions must intervene."

After failing to avoid the inevitable, Joseph Muscat tried to load the board of inquiry with Labour Party loyalists and limit its terms of reference, raising concerns about whether the government's efforts to find and bring to justice the masterminds who ordered Daphne's assassination were in fact genuine, or whether the inquiry would be nothing more than state-sponsored reputation washing. Two months of wrangling later, all parties finally agreed that chief justice emeritus Joseph Said Pullicino and judge Abigail Lofaro would serve on the inquiry, with justice emeritus Michael Mallia acting as chairperson.

When the hearings began, it quickly became evident why Muscat had done everything he could to obstruct them. In December 2020 the Parliamentary Assembly of the Council of Europe's special rapporteur Omtzigt wrote, "In a few months, the Daphne Caruana Galizia inquiry has done more to expose the corruption, misgovernment and criminal conspiracies that plagued Malta at the time of her death than all of the endless, opaque and ineffectual magisterial inquiries put together."

The police had always claimed they couldn't initiate corruption cases based on stories reported in the press, but when the Financial Intelligence Analysis Unit deputy director, Alfred Zammit, was called before the public inquiry, he admitted that they used Daphne's site as an open source for their investigations. The same could not be said of the police. Ian Abdilla, head of the Economic Crimes Unit, was forced to admit before an incredulous panel of judges that the police had done nothing about the Panama Papers. Keith Schembri and Konrad Mizzi weren't even called in for questioning.

"How could you not send for Keith Schembri and Konrad Mizzi?" judge Abigail Lofaro said. "We seem to be living in a parallel universe."

Abdilla didn't send an official request for information to Panama either, and he didn't bother asking Montenegro for information at all. As for the men who set up the Panama company structures—and so much else—NexiaBT directors Brian Tonna and Karl Cini, Abdilla admits he only spoke to them during the Egrant inquiry.

He did seek information from Dubai in December 2018, but Malta's request was ignored because Abdilla sent them the wrong bank account number. Was it a deliberate omission meant to sabotage the case? The stalled investigation allowed Yorgen Fenech to take two checks worth €1.5 million out of his company in April 2019 when the UAE unfroze the account after Malta failed to follow up.

Abdilla finally did set out to question Fenech after the press exposed the Electrogas CEO as the owner of 17 Black, but Deputy Police Commissioner Silvio Valletta phoned and told him to call it off because Fenech wasn't feeling well. Abdilla said he didn't ask how Valletta knew this or whether the two were friends. Asked why he chose to visit Fenech's apartment rather than call him in for questioning, Abdilla told the court, "He wasn't a person of interest."

"The police always bring the person to the depot to be questioned," judge Michael Mallia said. "He goes, not you!"

As for Silvio Valletta—the top police official who vacationed with Fenech and kept him informed of the progress of the murder investigation—he claimed that he received a phone call from Keith Schembri that same day. "Is this what you do?" Joseph Muscat's right-hand man had asked him. "Investigate from allegations in a newspaper?"

Lawyer Therese Comodini Cachia cut in. "So the chief of staff was superior?"

"He was the chief of staff of the prime minister," Valletta replied. "I had to answer him and give him the information he was asking from me."

"Did you never tell him you were the police and it's not his business?" Lofaro asked. She asked whether it was normal for the chief of staff of a prime minister to call a police commissioner. Had he ever seen this before in his twenty years of experience?

Valletta confirmed that he had not. He also said it was the first time the Office of the Prime Minister had requested briefings on the progress of a police investigation. "Dr. Muscat wanted that."

The head of the Economic Crimes Unit wasn't alone in choosing to look the other way while Joseph Muscat's closest collaborators allegedly laundered money like an Iranian banker with two bulging bags and a private jet. Toward the end of the sitting, judge Joseph Said Pullicino asked whether Abdilla's total inaction had anything to do with written advice from Attorney General Peter Grech "to tread very carefully on the Panama Papers, because there was trouble brewing in the country." The judge was referring to a document found in an Economic Crimes Unit file. "Was that why you did nothing?" he asked.

Abdilla claimed he didn't remember.

In another written note, dated May 16, 2016, the attorney general advised police that it would be "highly intrusive" to follow through on the Financial Intelligence Analysis Unit's suggestion to seize evidence from NexiaBT's servers. Grech said it would carry a considerably high legal risk that could be "counterproductive."

Even a casual perusal of the published material reveals the central role NexiaBT played in setting up the offshore entities for Joseph Muscat's two top men, but when the much-derided former police commissioner took the stand, he confirmed to the board that he too had done nothing.

"During my time as commissioner of police, a file on the Panama Papers was not opened. First you gather evidence," Lawrence Cutajar insisted, "then you call people in."

Judge Michael Mallia was incredulous. "You spent a whole year after the publication of the Panama Papers doing nothing."

"The police were waiting for documentation from the banks.

Before questioning a person, you need the evidence in hand for the disclosure."

Judge Said Pullicino cut in, explaining to the career law enforcement officer that he could have questioned a person of interest before pressing charges.

"Why didn't you go for the servers of NexiaBT?" Lofaro said.

"Evidence is being collected."

As the testimony became heated, Mallia said, "Our concern is the fact that you received the report from the FIAU [Financial Intelligence Analysis Unit] and the documents in the public domain, and the only person whom you could have progress with, you didn't send for."

The ex-commissioner had been a national laughingstock since he chose to enjoy a rabbit dinner with friends rather than secure evidence in Malta's most shocking political scandal. Asked about the fateful night that had forever branded him the Bunny Nibbler, Cutajar continued to defend his inaction. "How can I go to the attorney general when his advice was that there wasn't an underlying criminal offense but just writing on a blog?"

"When a blog gives you certain information which cannot be obtained except from the bank, you have circumstantial evidence," Mallia replied. "This all pointed to one outcome, and you discarded it."

"Pardon me, but the theory that you send for a person and then try to collect the evidence doesn't make sense. You need evidence in hand so that if the person doesn't cooperate—"

"You had evidence," an angry Mallia said. "You had the servers!"

Like so many other government officials, Cutajar's excuse was that he was just following orders.

"Nobody's perfect," he said, "but if there is something which I did nothing wrong in it was this—you do not take action contrary to the advice you are given."

• • •

Top police officials weren't alone in failing to take action. Every government official who testified before the public inquiry showed alarming symptoms of memory loss compounded by temporary blindness—especially those closest to the center of power. The standard reply used by present and former staff at the Office of the Prime Minister was "I don't remember" or "I don't know" or "but I'm a person of trust."

"Why are you paid if you gave no input?" Mallia said. "How is it possible that you were between four walls and you heard nothing?"

It seems the only responsibility everyone could agree to take action on was cashing their own paycheck.

Towering above them all, pulling strings like a puppet master, was the most rotten sector of all: Malta's elected representatives. Each politician who testified said the same things, and most pointed a finger at Konrad Mizzi.

Finance Minister Edward Scicluna—the man responsible for guarding the public purse—blamed the prime minister's inner circle, referring to it as a "kitchen cabinet" that made the real decisions. "Everyone knows about the closeness of Keith Schembri and the then-prime minister," he said. "They were one and the same team.

"There were a lot of explanations and attempts at explaining away what happened," Scicluna said, referring to Muscat's refusal to remove Schembri and Mizzi after they appeared in the Panama Papers. "The majority of the parliamentary group were advising the PM to distance himself." Scicluna claimed he had insisted that the two step down, but when the opposition called for a vote of confidence in parliament, all those ministers who told the inquiry they'd demanded resignations in private backed Mizzi in parliament with their vote—including the finance minister. "It was either vote in favor or resign," he said, justifying his decision by pointing out that he'd left a lucrative job in Brussels to enter local politics. "Why should I resign if someone else did wrong?"

The minister who held the government purse strings and controlled fiscal expenditures blamed structural deficiencies for his "inability" to do anything about the powerful lawyers and consultants who seemed to be leading negotiations on major projects like Electrogas and the Vitals Global Healthcare deal that turned over public hospitals to a known fraudster. "Whoever wants to hijack a system, it is that person who is responsible," Scicluna said. "I am not."

When he was finally pushed out of the Finance Ministry under Joseph Muscat's successor, Scicluna became governor of the Central Bank of Malta, despite being under criminal investigation for his role in the public-private hospitals partnership. The previous governor earned €89,000 per year, a package the contract said would remain the same for the full five-year term. Scicluna bumped this up to €100,000 in a surprise pay raise and then took the former governor's job. The man he replaced was given the freshly invented role of special commissioner for economic, financial, and trade relations with the United Kingdom at the same €100,000 salary. When he moved to the bank, Scicluna took along his entire staff, including his political canvasser-turned-chauffeur and his personal secretary, paying the seasoned professionals who once held those jobs to do "other duties." According to his tax return, the seventy-four-year-old was also raking in over €52,000 in "pensions, interest and dividends," including three taxpayer-funded pensions—one for his time as an MEP and two local pensions, including the normal social security pension paid to anyone over age sixty-two.

Every official had a similar story to tell. They weren't responsible for any of the dark deals that spread through all levels of government under the former prime minister. They saw nothing and heard nothing. They simply cashed their checks and minded their own ministerial backyards.

As minister for home affairs, Michael Farrugia was responsible for the police and the security services, but he claimed to know nothing about corruption allegations that plagued every major government project. "My role is to give police all the necessary tools," he said, "not to investigate." He didn't even know if police were investigating Konrad Mizzi and Keith Schembri, the two top officials exposed in the Panama Papers. When asked whether he was aware that Muscat's chief of staff attended briefings by police and the security services on the progress of the Caruana Galizia murder investigation, Farrugia again claimed ignorance, saying he didn't ask. "That was part of the prime minister's remit. I bore my own responsibility."

Farrugia claimed he had been unaware of decisions taken by his government—including decisions on issues that fell under his responsibility—insisting cabinet members were only provided with "concept and principles" for major projects like Electrogas. They were never shown the contracts others signed in their name.

Judge Joseph Said Pullicino said, "It's always the same story." Having a cabinet that doesn't vet transparency is the "yeast for corruption."

"Nobody should expect cabinet to vet a lengthy contract and all its details," Farrugia said. "That's for the relative minister, the permanent secretary, and all related structures to do." If any "concrete evidence" of wrongdoing was found, he would be the first to support taking action against it, but "there needs to be concrete proof, and then action should be taken."

The same line of reasoning had been used since 2016 to defend inaction by the authorities, despite ample published evidence of wrongdoing. As for Mizzi and Schembri, the minister formerly responsible for police couldn't confirm Joseph Muscat's standard claim that the two men were being investigated, and therefore no action could be taken against them "until the outcome of the magisterial inquiries."

A few politicians threw others under the bus, but throughout it all one thing was abundantly clear: all roads led back to Muscat. Despite the former prime minister's attempts to claim he was betrayed by those he trusted too much, even Keith Schembri told the public inquiry, "I never did anything behind the prime minister's back."

Schembri made several other surprising revelations during his grueling six-hour hearing. He admitted that he knew about the leak of Electrogas documents months before Daphne's murder, something Electrogas claimed it only found out about in December 2017, two months after her death. He also admitted that the 2017 snap election had nothing to do with Daphne's claim that Michelle Muscat owned Egrant, the third Panama company set up at the same time as Schembri's and Mizzi's, despite the disgraced former prime minister testifying that it was the reason for his decision. Schembri said he and Muscat had actually begun planning for an early election in February or March 2017. Yorgen Fenech claimed to have known the date in 2016, and testimony from middleman Melvin Theuma revealed that the plot to assassinate Daphne was briefly put on hold pending the outcome of the vote.

In the end, the public inquiry board's long-awaited four-hundred-plus page report found the Maltese state responsible for Daphne's death. By creating a climate of impunity where corrupt ministers were protected, where regulatory and law enforcement institutions were toothless, and where business interests colluded with politicians to promote lucrative large-scale projects regardless of whether they were in the public interest, former prime minister Joseph Muscat presided over impunity that "like an octopus spread to other entities like regulatory institutions and the police, leading to the collapse of the rule of law."

The inquiry found evidence "that powerful elements in public administration could have been involved in illegal activity which was the primary focus of the investigations of the murdered journalist." Such activity included "abundant proof of excessive closeness and intrigue between elements of public administration at the highest levels and influential businessmen interested in promoting large development projects."

Rather than lead to heightened protection, the political reaction to Daphne's investigations was a sustained campaign of personal attacks led by representatives of the state that included denigration, hatred, and legal action aimed at her finances. The plan "was centrally organized from the office of the prime minister," led by member of parliament and party whip Glenn Bedingfield, a close personal friend of Muscat's who ran a blog dedicated to attacking Daphne while working at the prime minister's communications office. The unrepentant MP defended his actions before the public inquiry as "an equal and opposite reaction" to Caruana Galizia's writing.

"This direct confrontation reached its peak after the publication of the Panama Papers and the external circumstances surrounding the setting up of the foreign company known as 17 Black, when it became obvious that the journalist had obtained and was still receiving information that was most sensitive," the public inquiry report said.

The government began treating Daphne as the only opposition in the country, and the "confrontation escalated up until the point at which she was assassinated." The hired killers were so sure they'd get away with it that they bragged about "their contacts with ministers, the chief of staff, and other persons at the heart of power," referring to them in court as "no. 1," "the old man," and "the king."

"It is certain that they had been or felt like they were assured that they would be protected by those who wished to silence the journalist the most," the report stated.

Their confidence was not misplaced. Even after the murder, high-ranking police officials and public authorities acted "in a manifestly illicit way, if not illegally" to assist suspects by deflecting journalists from the details that were being uncovered.

Far from blaming everything on Muscat's inner circle, the public inquiry found the entire cabinet "collectively responsible" for Daphne's death. By failing to act when corruption story after corruption story was reported in the media, the ministers gave "silent approval" to the impunity at the heart of the administration.

Muscat's successor, Robert Abela, was careful to distance himself from the board's findings, opening his official apology to the Caruana Galizia family with the words, "I was appointed prime minister after the public inquiry into the murder started." When asked whether he would demand resignations, Abela said all members of government who had been mentioned were removed from their posts long ago. His obvious refusal to account for members of his own cabinet who were also part of Muscat's was a clear indication that any reforms enacted as a result of the inquiry would not be a threat to the individuals implicated in it.

"We are used to working in a highly divided, polarized society, but we never expected a journalist could be killed," Caroline Muscat said at a conference organized by Reporters Without Borders after the inquiry's report came out. "Unfortunately, what happened to Daphne could still happen today."

As a columnist, I was mostly isolated from the threats faced by *The Shift*'s investigative journalists. At worst, my weekly satire resulted in furious phone calls from a minister's aide who threatened to sue for libel because my description of his boss's foolish behavior hit uncomfortably close to home.

I saw many faces come and go during those first three years. They showed up fresh from university, idealistic, eager to report the news, only to be bludgeoned by hate mail and lawsuits from powerful people in government in response to honest reporting. I had a glimpse of the daily pressure they were under during a week of in-person meetings with Caroline on Gozo, Malta's sister island, in June 2019. We were supposed to be holed up in a quiet farmhouse, working on a fundraising plan to survive another year, but three government ministers had taken exception to *The Shift*'s reporting of their role in a public-private hospital partnership that robbed the country of some €7 billion, and they were attacking Caroline in court. Her phone never stopped ringing. I saw the rants, the arguments with lawyers, her anxious glances at the cash reserves, and the nervous exhaustion of trying to do an honest job while living under constant threat. When she ignored frantic calls from one member of parliament, the guy tried to pressure her by calling her mother. Rather than make an annual business plan, I spent most of that weeklong Gozo retreat editing articles and trying to come up with fundraising schemes to survive another SLAPP (strategic lawsuit against public participation) designed to kill the investigation by bankrupting the publisher.

Other attempts to silence stories took the form of distributed denial-of-service attacks that tried to knock *The Shift*'s website offline by overwhelming our server with a flood of simultaneous requests from a network of computers connected to a botnet. These cyberattacks always coincided with the publication of major investigations into government corruption.

# THE
# AFTERMATH

Labour needed not just a deep-cleaning exercise but an enema. Malta had hit bottom in so many ways, and all it took was one overinflated ego to bring it crashing down.

The new prime minister, Robert Abela, began his reign with token changes, dismissing Muscat's puppet police commissioner and refusing to appoint Konrad Mizzi or Chris Cardona as ministers. But the others were still there, forming Malta's largest ever cabinet, and back-bench MPs were still being given government contracts to pad their pay and buy their loyalty.

Weeks after he took over, Abela nominated Konrad Mizzi as Malta's representative to the Organization for Security and Co-operation in Europe. Public outrage resulted in immediate withdrawal, but this only revealed the new prime minister's weakness. The outrage hadn't even died down when the story of Mizzi's €80,000 "consulting" contract hit the news. It turns out he hadn't resigned in disgrace in December when the entire cabinet tried to distance themselves from the pariah in the room to save their own skins. No, he actually got a raise in the form of a tourism consultancy courtesy of Joseph Muscat.

The disgraced former prime minister had also taken care of his chief of communications, Kurt Farrugia. The man who accompanied

Muscat, Schembri, and Mizzi on their secret trip to Azerbaijan was made head of Malta Enterprise at a cost to taxpayers of €130,000 a year, topping out at €180,000 over the nine-year contract. Farrugia would get a tax-free €130,000 if he decided to quit and €250,000 if he was fired by Muscat's successor.

The only member of the inner circle to face any sort of justice was Keith Schembri. He was indicted for money laundering and other financial crimes in relation to an illicit deal that happened before the 2013 election, raising questions over whether these relatively minor charges were filed in order to give international institutions the impression that investigations into corruption were progressing. Unfortunately, further questioning was put on hold as Schembri underwent medical treatment for what the newspapers were calling an aggressive brain tumor. It was his second battle with cancer.

After news of his illness was reported in the press, Schembri's mother wrote on Facebook, "How I wish I lived in a dictatorship where freedom of speech doesn't exist. They exploit freedom of speech to destroy families and speculate on people's health before the results have even come out yet." Labour Party trolls picked up on the post, flooding online comment boards and discussion forums with the narrative that reporting on Schembri's condition and its potential implications for the murder case was "taking pleasure in someone else's ill health," "bitter," "evil," and intended to "destroy families." His potentially terminal diagnosis raised serious questions over whether justice would ever be achieved for Daphne and her family. Would the truth come out if the man at the center of suspected state involvement was unable to be investigated or charged?

As for Joseph Muscat, he changed the policy on terminal benefits right before he was run out of office. His successor wouldn't say how Muscat amended it in 2018 and again in 2019, or what magic formula he used to pay himself three times more than the average of €37,000 given to other departing ministers. But the man the Organized Crime and Corruption Reporting Project named as 2019 Person of the Year in Organized Crime and Corruption walked away with a €120,000 golden handshake. Five days after he handed power to his successor, the freshly demoted backbench MP showed up as a lobby-ist for Steward Healthcare as they tried to secure additional taxpayer funding beyond the "sinister" secret contract Mizzi had negotiated for the three public hospitals they now controlled. At the time of this writing, Muscat is reportedly under investigation for a series of "consulting payments" he received soon after leaving office, from companies linked to the hospitals deal.

The trial of hitman brothers George and Alfred Degiorgio finally began in October 2022 after months of delayed court proceedings caused by their filing more than a hundred pretrial pleas and assorted pardon requests since the compilation of evidence against them began in December 2017. The prosecution's opening statement was followed by a lunch break that stretched to three hours as journalists waited anxiously in the courtroom to find out what this new delay might mean.

When the accused killers filed back into court late that afternoon, they shocked the nation by changing their plea to guilty. Given the weight of evidence against them, it was difficult to see how they could do otherwise. The two men had adamantly clung to their not-guilty plea throughout the five-year period leading up to this moment, re-fusing to utter a word under interrogation, until George Degiorgio appeared on a podcast hosted by Reuters journalist Stephen Grey. "It's fucking bullshit," he said on a phone call from prison. "They used us...they used us."

Degiorgio told Grey that the brothers had asked for €150,000 to kill Daphne, but he would have asked for €10 million if he'd known who she was. "For me it was just business," he said. "Business as usual."

And then he laughed. He also said there was much more to the story. "They don't want to hear us," he told the shocked journalist. "Do you believe this country, how fucking corrupt it is? We're not going down alone."

George and his brother Alfred were sentenced to forty years of imprisonment for their roles in Daphne's murder and ordered to pay tens of thousands of euros in legal costs and confiscated criminal proceeds. The two hitmen remain the only people successfully prosecuted for the assassination. Their accomplice, Vince Muscat, was given a reduced fifteen-year sentence in a plea bargain deal that saw him turn state's witness, and middleman Melvin Theuma was granted a presidential pardon after turning state's witness.

As of 2023 the accused mastermind, Yorgen Fenech, and the accused bomb makers, Robert Agius and Jamie Vella, remain in pretrial custody. More than six years after the assassination that shocked Europe, none of the politicians implicated in Daphne's killing have been arrested or charged.

In Malta under Joseph Muscat's successor, it's all business as usual. The only attempts Robert Abela made to rein in corruption came as a result of intense pressure from abroad, and even those were minimal and riddled with deliberate loopholes. The international community responded by imposing clear sanctions to further isolate the country from the global financial system.

Online gaming—worth some 13 percent of GDP—was shaken by repeated money-laundering scandals, all uncovered by Italian police rather than by the authorities in Malta, who seemed unwilling to take a closer look at an industry the Organized Crime and Corruption Reporting Project described as "the ATM for the Italian Mafia."

After being cut loose by Deutsche Bank and ING, Malta's flagship bank, the state-controlled Bank of Valletta, was unable to find a foreign institution willing to extend it U.S. dollar correspondent banking privileges. It had to rely on Western Union, the same company migrant workers used to remit funds to their families in Africa.

Joseph Muscat's lucrative citizenship-by-investment scheme was also under terminal pressure. When the European Union opened infringement proceedings against Malta to put an end to the contentious program, the government vowed to take the fight all the way to the European Court of Justice.

The most damaging blow fell in June 2021, when Malta was placed on the Financial Action Task Force's gray list of countries at high risk of money laundering and terrorist financing, a decision Prime Minister Robert Abela called "unjust" and "not deserved." It was the first and only European Union country to join global tax havens like Panama and the Cayman Islands, authoritarian Myanmar, and strife-torn Zimbabwe, Yemen, and Syria as the subject of increased monitoring by the anti-money-laundering watchdog. The government responded, not with promises to reform, but with accusations of "big countries bullying a small country."

Not long after the task force delivered the news, which shouldn't have shocked anyone in government, and despite frantic last-minute lobbying, the United Kingdom placed Malta on its list of high-risk countries for money laundering and terrorist financing, increasing the administrative burden of dealing with companies and individuals in Malta.

Sure enough, businesses started leaving at a rate of three a week, with forty-five financial services companies turning in their license to operate in Malta within the first few months. But this overt jumping ship was simply a more visible manifestation of the "shadow gray listing" that saw 616 companies relinquish various types of licenses from the Malta Financial Services Authority between 2018 and 2020.

Foreign residents began leaving, too, as an island once regarded as one of the world's top ten countries for expats was increasingly seen as one of the worst. This shift in perception was reflected in Malta's dramatic plunge down the rankings of the annual Expat Insider survey published by InterNations, a global expat network with some 4.2 million members worldwide: from fourth in 2015 to fiftieth out of fifty-nine countries in 2021.

None of this should have come as a surprise. The only surprise is that it didn't happen sooner.

# EPILOGUE

Joseph Muscat both embodied the law and transgressed it. His followers admired his cunning: often cornered but never caught, he was undefeatable at the polls. The prime minister's downfall felt catastrophic, as though an apocalypse of shame and repentance had been reached, but such emotions don't last long in the Mediterranean.

Would Malta change? I hoped so, for the sake of my friends, but history would indicate not. The web of corruption spread through every layer of society. Too many people would have to give up on too much easy access to power, or choose honesty over short-term gain and over the intense pressure of supporters who expected something in return for their vote. Everyone had a price for not objecting and for looking the other way.

A couple months before she was killed, Daphne wrote: "Maltese society is essentially criminal. That is how it grew and survived. Read your history. The last thing we need is to embrace it in the way we are doing now. If we continue to embrace criminality, to make excuses for it, to allow people in public life to wear two hats, to act as if there are no boundaries or standards, to understand that yes, some things really are black or white, then we might as well stop pretending, go the whole hog, and watch while all the decent young people fly out never to return—and Malta turns into 1930s Chicago (quite frankly, it's there already) or 1980s Palermo."

It was all so sad and so sordid. A talented, intelligent, uncompromising woman had died violently—and for what? The economy built on corruption will collapse, and Labour will be replaced by the Nationalist Party. The country will spend years rebuilding what they lost. A decade will pass, maybe more. Then they'll forget and do it all over again. Just as surely as Mintoff led to Muscat, Muscat will lead to a version much worse than himself, more ruthless and shameless, armed with the tools of the social media age. The roots of it all were deeply embedded in the culture. As Foreign Minister Evarist Bartolo told a shocked Tim Sebastian on DW's *Conflict Zone*, "The rule of family and the rule of friends is stronger than the rule of law."

A year before Daphne was killed, Malta felt like a plane in a steep dive, with the pilot pushing the throttle to full. I didn't want to be there when it hit the ground.

We'd moved to Malta because I was inspired by Lawrence Durrell's breezy Mediterranean vision, but the island's spirit of place exerted a malevolent influence, like radon gas silently poisoning a house. The heat induced an almost drunken ethical laxity and a loosening of personal morals. This slack attitude of "It doesn't affect me directly, so why care?" was interrupted by sudden acts of violence, brawls, stabbings, the occasional killing, and fights that quickly gave way to easy tears and forgetfulness. Life was a series of contradictions, logical fallacies, and self-destructive, shortsighted behavior that seemed to lack all reason. Oblivious outsiders bought into the postcard veneer—"It's like Disney Sea," said one Japanese expat—but Malta corrupted all of us, even those who tried to look away.

Those foreign residents who seemed to thrive despite the growing lawlessness kept up appearances, desperately polishing sailboats, hosting parties, and pretending to live a slice of the good life. Willful blindness was the price of the cut-rate Cannes they thought they were inhabiting. For the rest of us, lives gradually fell apart, marriages broke up, and otherwise decisive people vacillated and clung to excuses to justify hanging on for just one more year. Toward the end I was staying up all night, working out too hard, neglecting my business, and polishing off full bottles of wine as nihilism solidified to apathy, interrupted by brief episodes of rage. What comes to seem normal when living in such an inward-looking place is very strange when seen from outside. My wife and I would look back at it all months later and agree that we had escaped the island at exactly the right time.

Of course, it's easy to identify demarcation points in hindsight, and easy for those who survived to spot the moment it all went wrong. But those immersed in such a situation have a tendency to just live through it, to try to maintain their ordinary lives for as long as they can. Only a handful of people seemed to realize life could not continue down that path.

Our trips abroad grew longer as the political situation got worse in the wake of the Panama Papers. I wrote articles on assignment for a Canadian travel magazine. We spent a month in Tokyo in a short-let flat, two weeks in the Portuguese Algarve, and six weeks in the Baltics, working remotely and coming back to our Malta flat just long enough to swap a few books, do a few loads of laundry, and rest up for the next trip. We were testing the waters to see if any of these places would make a good residence, but none were appealing enough to take the leap despite the increasingly unpleasant living conditions, overcrowding, and noise that now beset the island. The ability to both save money and travel also made it difficult to break away. As a noncitizen who wasn't employed locally, I was only taxed on income sent to me in Malta—a fact I discovered when I submitted my first income tax return. Nowhere else in Europe could compete with that.

We didn't want to remain in Malta; we just failed to leave. And then one night in December 2016 we were offered the sublet on an *altbau* flat with creaking wooden floors in Berlin, provided we would move in three weeks. It was our favorite city in Europe, but given the local housing crisis we'd never considered it a realistic possibility. My online fitness publishing business had faded out by then, as all such businesses do, so moving to Germany would mean a return to the uncertainties of freelancing for me and a tech industry translation job for Tomoko.

We drove to a waterside bar where the proprietor poured good English beer to talk it over. He was serving roast beef and Yorkshire pudding, and a group of elderly British expats had dusted off their Sunday clothes and gathered together for a sense of home. There was something terribly melancholy about it all, an atmosphere of faded colonialism, of something lost that was smaller than a world but larger than a life.

When the glasses were drained, we took a short walk along the shore to look at the lights of the free port in the distance. Jan Morris wrote that Trieste had a "numen of regret." And what of Malta? It had a numen of decay, of shabbiness, of petty crookedness and dishonesty. The sea at night no longer had that peaceful feeling of Mediterranean harbor towns. It had an ominous stillness, a skulking quality that I associate with smugglers rather than commerce or leisure.

Had I idealized some sort of prelapsarian Malta that existed prior to Joseph Muscat, or was Pirate Island closer to the truth? Life there had worn me down, and I could no longer summon the energy to care.

In the end, we just slipped away. No one at the gym seemed to notice when I walked in and returned my key. The barber who had cut my hair every month for the past six years, and who I considered a friend, said, "Oh, well, good luck then," and that was it. Malta is a place where foreigners come and go. I wasn't expecting trumpets or open weeping, but it felt like my existence on the island was as transient and unimportant as I had intuited all along.

We spent a few days revisiting our favorite spots: Dingli Cliffs, the alleys of Birgu, and Valletta, especially Valletta. And we said our goodbyes to the handful of people who were sad to see us go. I guess you could call it a farewell tour.

We drank Armagnac all night with friends in Zejtun and raised a glass with the guys who ran our favorite wine shop. We visited the painter who wore fingerless gloves inside his house all winter like a tramp in a Dickens novel, and for the first time in our long acquaintance he spoke openly about politics and the dreadful depths his country had fallen into. We took coffee with another friend in Rabat, who gave us a bag of frozen *pastizzi* from her favorite shop, with instructions for how we should bake them. We thought of all the good things about our island life each time we bit into those crisp, oily, ricotta-stuffed treats, and memories and stories came flooding back. And we said our farewells to Dr. Dalli, knowing we would probably never meet again.

Then we sold the car, I packed up my books, and we boarded an Air Malta flight with one-way tickets at the beginning of January 2017.

I thought I'd feel nostalgic as I watched the island vanish below me for the last time. Malta is at its aerial best in winter, clad in green, with the bones of its hills poking through and pale stone houses jutting up like teeth. But it was an early flight, and all I felt was tired.

It's been more than six years since we left. I continue to write articles for *The Shift* and to pitch in with editing and running the newsroom when needed. I'll keep doing those things until the men who killed Daphne are prosecuted and jailed, because she didn't deserve to die for her writing, because we never got a chance to meet in person, and because I still can't get those crime scene photos out of my head.

# CAST OF CHARACTERS

**Abdilla, Ian**—Head of the police Economic Crimes Unit. Failed to act on the Panama Papers revelations and did not question politicians exposed for high-level corruption. Was later removed from the unit in June 2020 but remained assistant police commissioner.

**Abela, Robert**—Labour Party prime minister of Malta after the resignation of Joseph Muscat, for whom he had acted as legal adviser.

**Agius, Robert**—Accused alongside Jamie Vella of supplying the bomb used to kill journalist Daphne Caruana Galizia. Charged with complicity in the murder.

**Apap Bologna, Paul**—A director of and key investor in the Electrogas power station project. Owner of Kittiwake, a secret offshore company opened at the same time as Yorgen Fenech's 17 Black.

**Arnaud, Keith**—Chief police inspector in the Daphne Caruana Galizia murder investigation.

**Cardona, Chris**—Economy minister who froze journalist Daphne Caruana Galizia's bank account in a libel suit launched over allegations that he was seen in a German brothel while on government business. Linked to an alleged aborted 2015 plot to kill the journalist. Denies all involvement.

**Caruana Galizia, Daphne**—Investigative journalist killed with a massive car bomb on October 16, 2017. Had been investigating corruption at the highest levels of Malta's government during Prime Minister Joseph Muscat's tenure.

**Caruana Galizia, Matthew**—Son of murdered journalist Daphne Caruana Galizia and a data journalist who shared a Pulitzer Prize for his work with the International Consortium of Investigative Journalists on the Panama Papers.

**Cini, Karl**—Partner in the accounting firm NexiaBT that opened secret offshore companies for Chief of Staff Keith Schembri and Energy Minister Konrad Mizzi within days of the 2013 election.

**Cutajar, Lawrence**—Malta police commissioner. Failed to investigate the Panama Papers revelations, refused to seize evidence from Pilatus Bank on the night Daphne Caruana Galizia published her Egrant allegation, and chose not to investigate any of the well-documented stories of high-level corruption she published. Was removed by Prime Minister Robert Abela in 2020 and given a lucrative government consulting contract.

**Degiorgio, Alfred**—Hitman convicted of planting the bomb that killed journalist Daphne Caruana Galizia. Accomplice of brother George Degiorgio and Vince Muscat. Was sentenced to forty years in prison.

**Degiorgio, George**—Hitman convicted of remotely detonating the bomb that killed journalist Daphne Caruana Galizia. Accomplice of brother Alfred Degiorgio and Vince Muscat. Was sentenced to forty years in prison.

**Fenech, Yorgen**—The richest man in Malta, heir to his family's Tumas Group of companies, and CEO of the Electrogas power station project. Owned the secret offshore company 17 Black, which was linked to offshore companies owned by Energy Minister Konrad Mizzi and Chief of Staff Keith Schembri. Was arrested while attempting to flee Malta in November 2019 and stands accused of commissioning the assassination of journalist Daphne Caruana Galizia.

**Grech, Peter**—Attorney general. Issued written advice to police "to tread very carefully on the Panama Papers" and advised police not to seize evidence from Pilatus Bank. Retired in September 2020.

**Hasheminejad, Ali Sadr**—Owner of Pilatus Bank. Was arrested in the United States in 2018 and convicted of bank fraud, but his conviction was later reversed under mysterious circumstances. Pilatus was shut down by the European Central Bank in November 2018.

**Mintoff, Dom**—Labour Party prime minister of Malta from 1955 to 1958 and 1971 to 1984. Was credited with introducing social benefits, social housing, and the separation of church and state. His second period in office was characterized by political violence, bomb attacks, widespread corruption, and economic hardship. Died August 20, 2012.

**Mizzi, Konrad**—Energy minister, health minister, and later tourism minister. Signed every corrupt deal entered into by Joseph Muscat's administration, including the Electrogas power station deal. Was exposed in the Panama Papers for opening a secret offshore company soon after the 2013 election.

**Muscat, Caroline**—Founder and managing editor of *The Shift*, an investigative news outlet launched in response to Daphne Caruana Galizia's assassination.

**Muscat, Joseph**—Labour Party prime minister of Malta from 2013 to 2019. Was driven from office in disgrace after the arrest of Yorgen Fenech and links between his own inner circle and Daphne Caruana Galizia's murder. Denies all involvement.

**Muscat, Vince**—Accomplice of hitmen Alfred and George Degiorgio. Acted as the lookout when the bomb was planted in Daphne Caruana Galizia's car. Was sentenced to fifteen years in prison in a plea bargain deal to provide information about the murder.

**NexiaBT**—Accounting firm run by Brian Tonna and Karl Cini that opened secret offshore companies for Chief of Staff Keith Schembri and Energy Minister Konrad Mizzi soon after the 2013 election. Was also involved in the Electrogas power station selection process and in other corruption stories exposed by Daphne Caruana Galizia.

**Schembri, Keith**—Prime Minister Joseph Muscat's chief of staff. Was exposed in the Panama Papers for opening a secret offshore company soon after the 2013 election. Is alleged to have passed Yorgen Fenech details about the murder investigation, and was accused by Fenech of being involved in commissioning it. Denies all involvement.

**17 Black**—Secret offshore company owned by Yorgen Fenech and linked to the Electrogas power station deal, a wind farm deal in Montenegro, and secret offshore companies owned by energy minister Konrad Mizzi and chief of staff Keith Schembri.

**Theuma, Melvin**—Middleman in the Daphne Caruana Galizia assassination. Claims he acted as go-between for Yorgen Fenech with the Degiorgio brothers in commissioning Caruana Galizia's murder. Was granted a presidential pardon in November 2019 after turning state's witness.

**Tonna, Brian**—Partner in the accounting firm NexiaBT that opened secret offshore companies for chief of staff Keith Schembri and energy minister Konrad Mizzi soon after the 2013 election. Was involved in the Electrogas power station selection process, and was charged with financial crimes related to an earlier deal with Schembri.

**Valletta, Silvio**—Deputy police commissioner. Vacationed with accused murder mastermind Yorgen Fenech at a time when Fenech was already the lead suspect and allegedly passed information about the murder investigation to Fenech's friend Keith Schembri. Resigned from the police force but was never charged.

**Vella, Adrian**—Keith Schembri's doctor. Was arrested after allegedly passing a note from Schembri to Yorgen Fenech soon after Fenech's arrest. The note purportedly included a script to frame Economy Minister Chris Cardona for Daphne Caruana Galizia's murder.

**Vella, Jamie**—Accused alongside Robert Agius of supplying the bomb used to kill journalist Daphne Caruana Galizia. Was charged with complicity in the murder.

# CHRONOLOGY

**APRIL 2011**

The author and his wife move to Malta and rent an old house in the village of Zejtun.

**MAY 2011**

Malta holds a referendum on the legalization of divorce.

**JULY 2011**

Arriva takes over the island's bus service.

**MARCH 2013**

The Labour Party wins the general election. Joseph Muscat becomes prime minister.

Karl Cini of accounting firm NexiaBT contacts Mossack Fonseca about setting up Panama companies and offshore trusts.

**APRIL 2013**

Enemalta issues a call for expressions of interest in the power station project.

**JULY 2013**

NexiaBT sets up secret Panama companies: Hearnville (Konrad Mizzi), Tillgate (Keith Schembri), Torbridge (Chen Cheng), and Egrant (whose owner is too sensitive to name by email).

**AUGUST 2013**

The author moves to an apartment in the village of Mosta.

**OCTOBER 2013**

Ali Sadr Hasheminejad applies for a banking license in Malta, which is granted three months later.

**DECEMBER 2013**

Electrogas wins the power station tender.

**DECEMBER 2014**

Joseph Muscat, Keith Schembri, Konrad Mizzi, and Kurt Farrugia take a secret trip to Azerbaijan. A second trip takes place months later.

**MARCH 2015**

The author moves to the village of Zurrieq.

**APRIL 2015**

Malta signs gas supply and power agreement deals with Electrogas.

**JUNE 2015**

Konrad Mizzi establishes a New
Zealand trust and transfers ownership
of Hearnville.

17 Black opens a bank account in
Dubai.

Joseph Muscat, Keith Schembri,
and Yorgen Fenech attend Pilatus
Bank owner Ali Sadr Hasheminejad's
wedding in Florence, Italy.

**JULY 2015**

The local agent behind the liquefied
natural gas tanker that will supply
the Electrogas power station transfers
$200,000 to 17 Black.

**AUGUST 2015**

The state guarantee for Electrogas
increases to €360 million.

**NOVEMBER 2015**

Azerbaijani national Rufat Baratzada
transfers $1.4 million to 17 Black.

**DECEMBER 2015**

Karl Cini tells Mossack Fonseca that
17 Black and Macbridge will be the
target clients for Mizzi and Schembri's
offshore companies, with expected incoming transfers of €150,000 a month.

**FEBRUARY 2016**

Mossack Fonseca sends bank account
opening forms to NexiaBT for Konrad
Mizzi and Keith Schembri.

**APRIL 2016**

The Panama Papers investigation is published on April 3, exposing Mizzi's and
Schembri's secret offshore companies.

Joseph Muscat removes Mizzi as
minister of energy and health, but he
remains tasked with implementing the
government's energy plans.

**NOVEMBER 2016**

The SIM cards used to detonate the
bomb that kills Daphne Caruana
Galizia are purchased.

**JANUARY 2017**

Electrogas is chosen as the winning
bidder in the power station project.

The author leaves Malta and moves
to Berlin. He comes into contact
with Daphne and begins an email
correspondence.

**FEBRUARY 2017**

Daphne posts a photo on her blog
of Keith Schembri, Joseph Muscat,
Konrad Mizzi, and former government
official John Dalli with the caption
"17 Black." She describes 17 Black as
"the company which those crooks use
to move money in and out of Dubai"
and claims Malta's Financial Analysis

Intelligence Unit and police commissioner are aware of this.

**MARCH 2017**

Police commissioner Lawrence Cutajar tells the press he sees no reason to investigate Mizzi or Schembri.

**APRIL 2017**

April 19: Daphne publishes a blog alleging that the owner of Egrant is Michelle Muscat, wife of the prime minister.

April 20: Ali Sadr Hasheminejad is filmed by NET TV leaving the side door of Pilatus Bank late at night with two heavy suitcases.

April 21: A private jet leaves Malta Airport at 3:30 a.m. for Baku, Azerbaijan, and then onward to Dubai. Hours later Joseph Muscat calls for a magisterial inquiry into the Egrant allegations. The terms of reference will be written by his personal lawyer.

Yorgen Fenech meets Melvin Theuma outside the Blue Elephant restaurant and asks him to contact hitman George Degiorgio because he wants to kill Daphne.

Theuma meets Alfred Degiorgio at the Busy Bee coffee shop to agree on a price for the murder.

The day after the meeting, Theuma receives a call from Sandro Craus, head of customer care at the Office of the Prime Minister. He is invited to Castille to meet Keith Schembri and then directed to another office where he is given €1,200 a month for a phantom job.

The author publishes the first in a series of guest articles on Daphne's *Running Commentary* blog.

**MAY 2017**

On May 1 Joseph Muscat calls a snap election one year before the end of his term.

Yorgen Fenech tells Melvin Theuma to put the murder contract on hold.

**JUNE 2017**

Joseph Muscat's Labour Party wins reelection on June 3 with an even larger majority.

Hours after the result is announced, Yorgen Fenech tells Melvin Theuma to go ahead with the murder.

Two weeks later Fenech hands Theuma €150,000 in a brown envelope. Theuma gives €30,000 to the Degiorgio brothers and hides the rest at home.

**JULY TO SEPTEMBER 2017**

Alfred and George Degiorgio and Vince Muscat watch Daphne's home, track her movements, and plan the murder. They obtain a bomb from Robert Agius and Jamie Vella.

## OCTOBER 2017

Daphne Caruana Galizia is killed on October 16 with a massive car bomb.

Theuma meets Alfred Degiorgio at Ramla Taz-Zejtun and hands him €120,000 in cash plus €5,000 for expenses.

## NOVEMBER 2017

Caroline Muscat starts *The Shift*, an online investigative news portal.

George and Alfred Degiorgio and Vince Muscat are tipped off about a police raid to take place around December 5.

## DECEMBER 2017

Police raid the Marsa potato shed on December 4 and arrest the Degiorgio brothers and Vince Muscat.

Two days after the arrest, Joseph Muscat opens a WhatsApp group with Keith Schembri and Yorgen Fenech.

## APRIL 2018

Electrogas admits that they found a breach in their IT systems. Daphne's heirs confirm that she was working on a massive cache of Electrogas documents leaked to her by a whistleblower.

The Parliamentary Assembly of the Council of Europe appoints Pieter Omtzigt special rapporteur to monitor the progress of the murder investigation.

## MAY 2018

Concerned about his own safety, Melvin Theuma begins secretly recording his conversations with Yorgen Fenech.

## OCTOBER 2018

Police identify Yorgen Fenech as the likely murder mastermind. Joseph Muscat and Keith Schembri are informed.

## NOVEMBER 2018

The author meets Caroline Muscat in Berlin and begins writing weekly columns for *The Shift*.

On November 9 Reuters and the *Times of Malta* reveal that Yorgen Fenech owns 17 Black.

Fenech attempts to buy two grenades, a Glock pistol and silencer, two Scorpion submachine guns, and eight hundred rounds of ammunition on the dark web using five different cryptocurrency wallets.

On November 18 Melvin Theuma places twenty-eight calls to Fenech after media report that the murder mastermind has been identified.

## FEBRUARY 2019

Yorgen Fenech attends Joseph Muscat's private birthday party at the prime minister's official residence in Girgenti, with gifts worth tens of thousands of euros.

APRIL 2019

Yorgen Fenech tries to buy potassium
cyanide on the dark web.

JUNE 2019

The Parliamentary Assembly of the
Council of Europe votes in favor of
Pieter Omtzigt's call for an independent
public inquiry tasked with determining
whether the state facilitated Daphne's
murder or failed to prevent it.

The author travels to Malta and Gozo
for planning meetings with Caroline
Muscat.

SEPTEMBER 2019

Joseph Muscat's government gives in
to Council of Europe pressure and
announces the public inquiry.

NOVEMBER 2019

On November 14 Melvin Theuma is
arrested. He confesses to being the
middleman and turns state's witness in
exchange for a presidential pardon.

Joseph Muscat removes himself from
the WhatsApp group with Schembri
and Fenech after the *Times of Malta*
leaks news that "a major businessman"
is among the main suspects.

Fenech resigns from his directorships
of Electrogas and the family's Tumas
Group.

On November 20 Fenech is arrested
on his yacht while attempting to flee
Malta.

Under police interrogation, Fenech
claims Keith Schembri contributed
€80,000 to Daphne's murder. This information is not made public until the
following year during court testimony.

Enraged citizens stage a series of daily
protests outside parliament and the
prime minister's office.

On November 26 Joseph Muscat announces that Schembri has decided to
resign after a late-night meeting at Muscat's home. Schembri is arrested that
morning and taken in for questioning.
Konrad Mizzi resigns from the cabinet
later that day, and Economy Minister
Chris Cardona "suspends himself."

On November 29 Keith Schembri is
released from police custody with no
further questioning. Joseph Muscat
holds a late-night cabinet meeting
to discuss Yorgen Fenech's pardon
request. At a 3 a.m. press conference
he announces it was denied. Ministers
leave, but journalists are briefly detained
in the room by Labour Party thugs.

DECEMBER 2019

Nightly protests continue in Valletta,
growing in size.

On December 1 Joseph Muscat
announces his resignation but says he
will stay in office until a successor is
chosen on January 12.

On December 6 the public inquiry holds its first hearing.

On December 27 Muscat flies to Dubai for a seventy-hour "family holiday" followed by a quick trip to London.

## JANUARY 2020

On January 13 Robert Abela, an obscure backbench MP and former legal adviser to Joseph Muscat, becomes prime minister.

## JULY 2020

Melvin Theuma is found with his throat cut and six stab wounds to his abdomen the night before he is due to testify. He survives. Police and Theuma insist the injuries were self-inflicted.

## FEBRUARY 2021

On February 23 Vince Muscat admits his role in Daphne Caruana Galizia's murder and agrees to testify against the Degiorgio brothers in exchange for a plea bargain deal of fifteen years in jail.

Robert Agius and Jamie Vella are charged with supplying the bomb that killed Daphne.

## JULY 2021

The public inquiry into the assassination of Daphne Caruana Galizia finds the Maltese state responsible for her death.

## DECEMBER 2021

The U.S. State Department bans Konrad Mizzi, Keith Schembri, and members of their immediate families from travel to the United States "due to their involvement in significant corruption."

## OCTOBER 2022

In a last-minute plea reversal on the first day of their trial, George and Alfred Degiorgio admit to killing Daphne Caruana Galizia. They are sentenced to forty years in prison.

At the time of this writing, no politicians have been charged in connection with the murder.

# FURTHER READING

Details about the many cases of political corruption in Malta, the plot to kill Daphne Caruana Galizia, and the court cases and public inquiry can be found in Daphne's *Running Commentary* blog, *The Shift*, the *Times of Malta*, and the *Malta Independent*. The *Times of Malta* is also a useful source for articles on the Mintoff period and other historical interludes.

Reports dealing with the rule of law in Malta during Joseph Muscat's tenure are available online from the European Parliament (EP), the Parliamentary Assembly of the Council of Europe (PACE), the Group of States against Corruption (GRECO), and the Committee of Experts on the Evaluation of Anti–Money Laundering Measures and the Financing of Terrorism (MONEYVAL).

The books and articles listed below will also be helpful for readers interested in learning more about Malta.

Banfield, Edward C. *The Moral Basis of a Backward Society.* New York: Free Press, 1958.

Boissevain, Jeremy. *Factions, Friends, and Feasts: Anthropological Perspectives on the Mediterranean.* New York: Berghahn Books, 2013.

———. *Saints and Fireworks: Religion and Politics in Rural Malta.* London: Athlone Press, 1965.

———. "Why Do the Maltese Ask So Few Questions?" *Education* 3, no. 4 (1990): 16–23.

Camilleri, Mark. *A Materialist Revision of Maltese History, 870–1919.* Hamrun: SKS, 2016.

Cassar, Carmel. *A Concise History of Malta*. Msida: Mireva, 2000.

Cavaliero, Roderick. *The Last of the Crusaders: The Knights of St. John in the Eighteenth Century*. London: I. B. Tauris, 2009.

Fenech, Natalino. *Fatal Flight: The Maltese Obsession with Killing Birds*. London: Quiller Press, 1992.

Gauci, Liam. *In the Name of the Prince: Maltese Corsairs, 1760–1798*. Kalkara: Heritage Malta, 2016.

Hull, Geoffrey. "Late Medieval Maltese Surnames of Arabic and Greek Origin." *Symposia Militensia* 11 (2015): 129–43.

Mitchell, Jon P. *Ambivalent Europeans: Ritual, Memory, and the Public Sphere in Malta*. London: Routledge, 2002.

Raineri, Luca. "The Malta Connection: A Corrupting Island in a Corrupting Sea?" *European Review of Organized Crime* 5, no. 1 (2019): 10–33.

Thake, Conrad. "Interpreting the Landscape of the Maltese Islands." *Traditional Dwellings and Settlements Review* 5, no. 2 (Spring 1994): 37–47.

Wettinger, Godfrey. *Aspects of Daily Life in Late Medieval Malta and Gozo*. Msida: Malta University Press, 2015.

———. "Did Christianity Survive in Muslim Malta?" *Sunday Times of Malta*, November 19, 1989.

———. "Malta in the High Middle Ages." *Melita Historica* 15, no. 4 (2011): 367–90.

**Ryan Murdock** is the author of *Vagabond Dreams: Road Wisdom from Central America* and editor-at-large (Europe) for *Outpost*, Canada's national travel magazine. He shares his love of travel literature through the *Personal Landscapes* podcast and writes regularly for *The Shift*, an independent Maltese news portal. He lives in Berlin.